MIMESIS
INTERNATIONAL

PHILOSOPHY
n. 44

WITTGENSTEIN AND MARX

Language, Mind and Society

Edited by
Pietro Garofalo, Christoph Demmerling
and Felice Cimatti

MIMESIS
INTERNATIONAL

The volume was published with the contribution of the Project PRIN 2017 N. 201794A3F2_004, title "Designing effective policies for Politically Correct: A rhetorical/pragmatic model of total speech situation", CUP H24I17000330001, resp. Prof. F. Cimatti, Department of Political and Social Sciences.

CONTENTS

INTRODUCTION

What could the father of historical materialism and one of the main exponents of analytical philosophy have in common? If we consider the analytical and Marxist debates, the answer seems to be quite expected: not too much!

Wittgenstein was interested in logic and language his whole life and his early work has influenced those philosophers and scientists of Vienna's circle who were more focused on topics related to the philosophy of science. Even if in his mature works his approach to the study of language changed, it has never been considered as historically characterized, and even the language games that he analysed refer to simple situations in which there is no place for the consideration of political and economic conditions. More generally, according to what some of his students said, he was not interested in these topics at all. At first glance, Wittgenstein's most important political commitment was his decision to participate in the First World War, but even in this case it was more of an ethical reason than a political one, as his diaries written during the war testify: "If it is all over with me now, may I die a good death, mindful of myself. May I never lose myself! Now I might have the opportunity to be a decent human being, because I am face to face with death. May the spirit enlighten me" (McGuinnes, 1988, p. 221).

On the contrary, Marx was not only – like Hegel – a philosopher interested in politics, but he was, along with Engels, the most important point of reference for the communist movement of his period.

His political commitment led him to the detailed study of political economy and therefore many scholars and economists, who are not Marxists, consider him as one of the most important exponents of the Ricardian link. It is quite usual to think of the early Marx as a young philosopher influenced by Feuerbach and Hegel, while at the same time considering the late Marx as the prophet of the falling rate of profit who overcame philosophy. From this point of view his most important opponents have discussed Marx's theory of value, depicting, as noted by

Rubin, the paragraph of the fetisishm of commodities: "as an independent and separate entity, internally hardly related to Marx's economic theory. They present it as a supplement to the theory of value, as an interesting literary-cultural digression which accompanies Marx's basic text" (Rubin, 1973, p. 4).

If we consider how Marx often has not been read as a philosopher as such, it is not surprising that he was ignored within philosophy of language and within the philosophical debate on materialism, given that his 'materialism' was reduced to a problematic scientific conception of history.

Even if we look at the main philosophical texts they read, Marx and Wittgenstein seem to be poles apart. Marx always recognised a strong debt to Hegel, despite being controversial, and Wittgenstein to the most fierce enemy of the philosopher of Stuttgart, that is, Schopenhauer.

At first sight, the only point of contact seems to be their *apparent* "strength": the unsystematic approach to philosophy and the amount of pages written without the intention of publishing them.

Is there anything else to add?

Exactly forty years ago, in 1981, David Rubinstein wrote a book with the suggestive title "Marx and Wittgenstein, Social praxis and social explanation". From what has been said above, it should not amaze us that Rubinstein started his pioneering work by noting in the introduction how such parallelism "has never, to my knowledge, been attempted" (Rubinstein 1981). However, upon reading the book, the impression is that these two, apparently so distant authors, have many similarities. In recent decades, the comparison between these two great and radical philosophers has often seduced scholars of different countries and they have tried to highlight the various and structural similarities concealed behind their great differences. In Rubinstein's work, the standpoint was the consideration that Marx and Wittgenstein proposed two similar philosophical conceptions about man in opposition to the Cartesian dualism of mind and body. Even if using different argumentations and in a different philosophical framework, both philosophers have not only defended a monist approach to the human being, but have also conceived the human being as a corporeal, sensitive creature and above all as a social entity. Moreover, the few but very dense Marxian passages dedicated to the problem of language seem to anticipate, or at least are similar, to Wittgenstein's critique of private language and to the key role recognised by the social conditions in order to determine the meanings of our words. Moreover, according to both philosophers, human mind and consciousness may not be reduced to the private and intimate sphere of the individual, but has to be understood as a social product of human (inter)actions.

Rubinstein's attempt has thus contributed a decisive role in deepening this comparison. However, in 2002, Kitching and Pleasants, in the introduction of another very important book on this topic, entitled "Marx and Wittgenstein: knowledge, morality and politics", stated how "overall what impresses one most about 'Marx and Wittgenstein' literature, apart from its sheer sparsity, is how little impact it has had on dominant understandings of Marx or Wittgenstein, either among Marxists or Wittgensteinians" (Kitching & Pleasants, 2002, p. 12).

Kitching and Plesants's book is surely a wider attempt at deepening the comparison between these two great philosophers as it contains different contributions that develop similarities between them, among which are some important contributions to the problem of language.

Moreover, in this book the important 1966 essay by Italian philosopher Ferruccio Rossi-Landi – with the suggestive title, "Towards a Marxian use of Wittgenstein"– was translated for the first time into English.

In reference to this debate, the contribution of the Italian philosopher is very important, because in contrast to Rubinstein, Rossi-Landi suggests that there are not only theoretical affinities between these two philosophers, but that these affinities are not accidental. Rossi-Landi brought to attention how the Marxist economist Sraffa – friend of Gramsci – had such an important influence on the 'second' Wittgenstein.

Rossi-Landi not only defended the thesis that the Wittgenstein of the *Philosophical Investigation* could be read in relation to Marxist thought, but also the more radical thesis, at least for that time, that Wittgenstein overcame his view presented in the *Tractatus*, where he proposed an analysis of the relationship between language and reality based on logical atomism and the 'picture theory', thanks to the influence of Marxism via the Marxist economist Sraffa, who was thanked by Wittgenstein himself in the Preface of the *Philosophical Investigations*: "Even more than to this— always certain and forcible— criticism I am indebted to that which a teacher of this university, Mr. P. Sraffa, for many years unceasingly practised on my thoughts. I am indebted to *this* stimulus for the most consequential ideas of this book." (Wittgenstein, 1958, p.viii)

This being said, we may question if the situation has changed over the last forty years. In recent years, many contributions have tried to deepen our understanding of the relationship between Marx and Wittgenstein, however, Marx's philosophy remains largely ignored within the philosophy of language's debate, as does Wittgenstein's similar thought within the field of political and social philosophy.

From this assumption the aim of this book arises, which, first of all contributes to the comparison from this particular view of the philosophy of language and mind, in order to highlight the strict relationship of these two research fields with politics and social philosophy. Secondly, it would contribute to not only stressing the potential of Marx's thought for philosophy of language, but also the political potential of some of Wittgenstein's concepts. Thirdly, it would be a contribution to the study and discussion of two authors who are always relegated to the background of the philosophical debate by the cognitive turn that has characterized the philosophy of mind and language of the last decades and that has so many points of contact with the affirmation of the social and political individualism in our contemporary societies.

Pietro Garofalo

Christoph Demmerling

Felice Cimatti

References

Kitching G., Pleasants N. (Eds.) (2002). *Marx and Wittgenstein. Knowledge, morality and politics*. New York: Routledge.

McGuinness B. (1988). *Wittgenstein: A Life: Volume I: Young Ludwig (1889–1921)*. London: Duckworth.

Rubinstein D. (1981). *Marx and Wittgenstein. Social Praxis and Social Explanation*. London: Routledge & Kegan Paul.

Rossi-Landi F. (1966). Toward a Marxian Use of Wittgenstein. In G. Kitching and N. Pleasants (Eds), *Marx and Wittgenstein; Knowledge, Morality and Politics*. London: Routledge, 2002, pp.185-212.

Rubin I.I. (1990). *Essays on Marx's theory of value*. Montréal-New York: Black Rose Book.

Wittgenstein L. (1958). *Philosophical Investigations*. Oxford: Basil Blackwell.

1.
HISTORICAL AND THEORETICAL SIMILARITIES

Moira De Iaco

THE PRESENCE OF MARX IN WITTGENSTEIN'S PHILOSOPHY OF LANGUAGE

1. *Introduction*

The idea of a relation between some aspects of Wittgenstein's philosophy and Marx's method is based on the network of Marxist contacts which has been created in Wittgenstein's life since the 1930s. We can suppose a Marxian influence on Wittgenstein's thought since his return to Cambridge in 1929, above all thanks to the Italian Marxist economist Piero Sraffa with whom Wittgenstein had an intense and fruitful, but also tormented attendance which went on with ups and downs from February of 1929 until the year before the philosopher's death (De Iaco, 2019). The Maxian network of Wittgenstein's interlocutors also includes Maurice Dobb, George Thomson, Nicholas Bachtin, and Fania Pascal with his husband Roy. Nevertheless, we could not claim that Wittgenstein was ever a Communist or a Marxist, although it seems that once he defines himself a Communist at heart (Monk, 1990). We will analyse the presence of Marx in Wittgenstein's philosophy in order to show that Wittgenstein's new anthropological way to look at philosophical problems after his return to Cambridge involves some analogies with the Marxian approach to phenomena, even though goals and outcomes of Wittgenstein's philosophy of language and Marx's thought remain different.

2. *Wittgenstein's Marxist network of relationship*

Fania Pascal, who taught Russian to Wittgenstein from 1934 to 1939, writes in her personal memory on Wittgenstein (Rhees and Wittgenstein, 1984) that in a period in which at Cambridge "all intellectuals sympathized with the left, Wittgenstein remained an old-fashioned conservative of the Austro-Hungarian empire". She also told that once Wittgenstein made an unpleasant comment on Marxism to which she replied saying that

"Marxism would never be discredit by his antiquated political ideas" (*ibid.*). It seems that Wittgenstein was perplexed about Fania's reply. Gakis (2015) highlights that Fania's husband was an active member of the Communist party and he edited the English edition of the first and second part of *The German Ideology* and of the *Theses on Feuerbach* and it could be possible that during the attendance of Fania's house Wittgenstein came into contact with the contents of these works.

Regarding Wittgenstein's political positions it has been affirmed that he was conservative (Rhees and Wittgenstein, 1984; Nyíri, 1982), or even anti-political: Fania wrote that he could not bear to talk about politics and Sraffa told Steinvorth (see De Iaco, 2018) that, in any case, Wittgenstein's political interpretation of what happened in the world was very naive. For instance, he was completely skeptical about the annexation of Austria to the Nazi regime: he was convinced that Austria was not necessary to Hiltler. As Sraffa told and Drury's testimony confirmed, Wittgenstein usually did not read newspapers: Sraffa informed him often about the fact of the world. However, according to Drury, Wittgenstein assumed a critical position toward Nazims and he was harsh when the Nazis came to power: he said that the country was now in the hands of a group of thugs and that he would not be surprised if they were witness of a witch hunt (Rhees and Wittgenstein, 1984). Furthermore, according to Gakis (2015, p. 925), Thomson told about "Wittgenstein's growing political awareness from the mid-1930s and onwards, his being kept informed about the current events and his sensitivity to the evils of unemployment and fascism and the growing danger of war".

In 1934 Wittgenstein planned to go to Russia with his friend Francis Skinner and, therefore, he started to take Russian lessons from Fania Pascal. Wittgenstein was fascinated by Russia because of his passionate readings of Dostoevsky's and Tolstoy's works (see McGuinness, 2013). In 1935 he got the visa for Russia by the Russian ambassador in London. Drury reported (Rhees and Wittgenstein, 1984) that in that period Wittgenstein talked to him about Lenin's philosophical writings saying that "they are absurd", but at least Lenin "wanted to do something with them". This testimony suggests that Wittgenstein knew in some extent Lenin's writings and he appreciated the pragmatism that characterizes them. In summer of 1935 Wittgenstein was in Russia and his stay there was for him so interesting and humanly rewarding that he thought of moving to Russia in 1937. It seems that he even received an offer of professorship at Moscow or Kazan university through Professor Janovskaya whom he met during his stay of 1935. Wittgenstein intended to accept the proposal, but he gave up moving because Germans in Russian became suspicious due to the political changes in Europe of those years (Sraffa, C/201).

Wittgenstein's attraction to Russia also comes from his friendship with the Marxian linguist Nicholas Bachtin who in 1936 had made the commitment to translate into Russian the book that Wittgenstein then imagined publishing (Wittgenstein, 2008, p. 258). Wittgenstein and Bachtin became acquaintances in Cambridge in 1930 where the linguist lived until 1935. Then, he lectured three years in Southampton before starting to lecture linguistics at the University of Birmingham. He was also an expert in classical literature, and he built by reading great philosophers like Nietzsche, Hegel, and Kant since an early age. Rothhaupt claims that Bachtin studied deeply Goethe, Splengler, and the ethnology focusing on the relationship between ordinary language and human life[1]. It seems to be confirmed by the notes on primitive points of view on language, magic, grammar, and popular etymology. During Bachtin's five years in Cambridge, as Fania Pascal reported (Rhees and Wittgenstein, 1984), Wittgenstein and his friend Francis Skinner attended the Bachtin's house and Nicholas Bachtin's wife claims that Wittgenstein and her husband used to have endless discussions. It seems that Wittgenstein drew well-being feeling by the intellectual exchange with Bachtin. In the early 1940s Wittgenstein and Bachtin met again. They reread together the *Tractatus*, thus Wittgenstein realized that his new thought was more understandable if compared with the previous one of the *Tractatus* (Wittgenstein, 2008, p. 258). According to Fania Pascal (Rhees and Wittgenstein, 1984), they probably also read Pushkin in Russian.

Rush Rhees was a pupil and a friend of Wittgenstein and he was a Socialist. In 1941 Rhees had read Max Eastman's book *Marxism: is it a Science?* that was published in 1935. Since we know (Wittgenstein, 2008) that, in 1944, Rhees and Wittgenstein had discussions, we can suppose that Rhees refers to his reading or to the contents of it during the meetings with Wittgenstein.

3. *A Marxian Influence on Wittgenstein's Philosophy via Sraffa*

Wittgenstein did not ever refer to Marx or to one of his works, but it is known that in the Thirties among his Marxian contacts circulated the English edition of *The German Ideology* of 1932. It seems that Sraffa

---

1   For this information I am indebted to Josef Rothhaupt that told me on April of 2015 about his investigations on Bachtin.

tried to convince Wittgenstein to read Marx, although Wittgenstein was reticence due to his opinion that Marx's language is illegible. According to Garegnani's testimony reported by Marjanović (2005), after a first refusal, Sraffa managed to persuade Wittgenstein who read the first book of *Capital*. We can suppose that this reading was probably always in its own way, that is not systematically, but by throwing an eye here and there. Rush Rhees also claims (Moran, 1972, p. 86) that Wittgenstein read parts of the first book of the *Capital*, but he may have read other works as well. In addition, Rhees affirms (*ibid.*) that Wittgenstein in the 1930s knew the fundamentals of dialectical materialism probably more through the discussions with Marxist friends than through direct reading of some Marx's writings. This statement of Rush Rhees about Wittgenstein's interest in dialectical materialism matches up to what Professor Yanovskaya reported telling of the meeting she had with Wittgenstein in Moscow in 1935 (*ibid.*, p. 88). Since Rhees was a socialist it could be possible that he discussed with Wittgenstein on topics such as Marx and Marxism. In this regard, Moran argued a deduction of Marxist ideas in Wittgenstein's mind when, in paragraph 284 of *Philosophical Investigations*, he speaks about a "transition from quantity to quality". Furthermore, it is possible to detect an incredible similarity between some Wittgenstein's ideas and passages from *The German Ideology*.

In fact, about the mental production we read in *The German Ideology* the following passage:

> The production of ideas, of conceptions, of consciousness, is at first directly interwoven with the material activity and the material intercourse of men — the language of real life. Conceiving, thinking, the mental intercourse of men at this stage still appear as the direct efflux of their material behavior. The same applies to mental production as expressed in the language of the politics, laws, morality, religion, metaphysics, etc., of a people. Men are the producers of their conceptions, ideas, etc., that is, real, active men, as they are conditioned by a definite development of their productive forces and of the intercourse corresponding to these, up to its furthest forms. Consciousness [*das Bewusstsein*] can never be anything else than conscious being [*das bewusste Sein*], and the being of men is their actual life-process. (Marx and Engels, 1998, p. 42)

And then a little further we find a direct reference to language:

> Only now, after having considered four moments, four aspects of primary historical relations, do we find that man also possesses "consciousness". But even from the outset this is not "pure" consciousness. The "mind" is from the

outset afflicted with the curse of being "burdened" with matter, which here makes its appearance in the form of agitated layers of air, sounds, in short, of language. Language is as old as consciousness, language is practical, real consciousness that exists for other men as well, and only therefore does it also exist for me; language, like consciousness, only arises from the need, the necessity of intercourse with other men. (*Ibid.*, p. 49)

According to Marx's thought which was influenced by Hegel, consciousness can only take form in language: language is the consciousness, self-produced in language. Consciousness is concrete and, since it is made up of language, it is shared with other men. All human spiritual production, from metaphysics to religion, law, and politics, is made up of language, more precisely, of the language spoken by a certain community. Therefore, we can say with Wittgenstein that in each language we find a popular philosophy, the stratified traditions and ways of life of some people: it means that we find the form of life, shared by the community which uses that language.

Then, in another passage of *The German Ideology* we find a surprising affinity between Marx and Engel's reasoning on the difficult task of philosophers and Wittgenstein's idea (1953, § 116) that philosophers must "bring words back from their metaphysical to their everyday use". Passages like the following ones, as Rossi Landi underlined (1966), arouse amazement in Wittgenstein's scholars and they trigger an inevitable comparison:

One of the most difficult tasks confronting philosophers is to descend from the world of thought to the actual world. Language is the immediate actuality of thought. Just as philosophers have given thought an independent existence, so they were bound to make language into an independent realm. This is the secret of philosophical language, in which thoughts in the form of words have their own content. The problem of descending from the world of thoughts to the actual world is turned into the problem of descending from language to life. (Marx and Engels, 1998, pp. 472-473)

A little further we can read:

The philosophers have only to dissolve their language into the ordinary language, from which it is abstracted, in order to recognise it as the distorted language of the actual world and to realise that neither thoughts nor language in themselves form a realm of their own, that they are only manifestations of actual life". (*Ibid.*, p. 473)

It resounds here the problem of the linguistic alienation of philosophy which makes its own language for its own speculations, transfiguring it. Philosophy forgets that the words which it uses are words of ordinary language that come from the actual life.

Despite these observed affinities, we have to highlight that, on one hand, we have Marx's philosophical thought that is intrinsically political because Marx is convinced that philosophy must transform the world, while on the other hand we have Wittgenstein who believes that philosophy cannot bring any progress to the thought and so it must limit itself to leave everything as it is. The aims of Wittgenstein's and Marx's philosophies are undoubtedly different, despite the interesting analogies we found in their writings.

There are scholars such as Rossi Landi (1966) and David Rubinstein (1981) who argued about a complementarity view of Marx's and Wittgenstein's thought. In this regard, according to Janik (1985, p. 139), Rubinstein claims that "Wittgenstein's contextualism and his peculiar emphasis upon social practice taken in conjunction with Marx's historical and economic analysis provide a sounder account of the *subject* that sociology should study". Furthermore, Rubinstein believes (*ibid.*) that "Wittgenstein's account of meaning in terms of 'forms of life' and his emphasis upon how traditional epistemological problems can be resolved by coming to comprehend social *practices*, instead of theoretically, is taken to complement the Marxian notion of praxis". Within the perspective outlined by Rubinstein, both for Wittgenstein and for Marx, as Janik writes, "the correct understanding of our actions makes the theoretical activity that provides fixed foundations for knowledge superfluous". By looking at men's actions it is possible to understand the phenomena of human life, since acting is at the origin of all human phenomena. The language also is born as an extension of human's primitive reaction and not from reasoning: language has from time to time flanked and sometimes replaced primitive behaviours providing us the possibility of acting by means of thought. The same goals of language are strictly practical. In this regard Wittgenstein writes (1953, § 491): "Not: 'without language we could not communicate with one another' — but for sure: without language we cannot influence other people in such-and-such ways; cannot build roads and machines, etc. And also: without the use of speech and writing people could not communicate".

The new Wittgenstein's way to look at the language in its relations to real life starting from the Thirties, after his return to Cambridge and, as we can say, to the 'official philosophy', is a phenomenological way insofar it foresees to *look through* language uses in order to convert the metaphysical meanings of words into everyday meanings. Therefore, in paragraph 116 of *Philosophical Investigations* we read: "When philosophers use a word — 'knowledge', 'being', 'object', 'I', 'proposition', 'name' — and try to grasp the *essence* of the thing, one must always ask oneself: is the word ever actually used in this way in the language-game which is its original home? — What *we* do is to bring words back from their metaphysical to their everyday use". In the first stage of his thought after his return to Cambridge, Wittgenstein was attracted to the construction of a primary/phenomenological language to remedy the shortcomings of his theory of language formulated in the *Tractatus*. Although he gave up this project that we find in *Philosophical Remarks*, he maintained its phenomenological instance according to which he continued to consider grammar as «the descriptive science of speaking» (Wittgenstein, 2000) in opposition to the science of thinking which tries to explain the phenomena and he assigned to philosophy the critical task of detecting misleading analogies in language uses (*ibid.*).

The new Wittgenstein's method to do philosophy is, as he writes in paragraph 109 of *Philosophical Investigations*, do not "advance of any kind of theory". Wittgenstein claims that

> we must do away with all *explanation,* and description alone must take its place. And this description gets its light, that is to say its purpose, from the philosophical problems. These are, of course, not empirical problems; they are solved, rather, by looking into the workings of our language, and that in such a way as to make us recognize those workings: *in despite of* an urge to misunderstand them. The problems are solved, not by giving new information, but by arranging what we have always known. Philosophy is a battle against the bewitchment of our intelligence by means of language.

In this regard, Wittgenstein used efficaciously the concept of praxis in 1936 in a note published in *Eine philosophische Betrachtung.* He writes: «An enormous amount of our philosophical problems is created by representing the praxis of our language in a false simplification» (Ms-115, 262, my transl.). In 1936, and in particular in *Eine philosophische Betrachtung*, we find many occurrences of the word "praxis". Due to this consistent use of it in the writings of 1936, it was thought that 1936 was the year in which Wittgenstein introduced the concept of praxis into his thought. Lo Piparo (2010), furthermore, on the basis of this data claimed a Gramscian derivation via Sraffa of the use of praxis in Wittgenstein's philosophy. Actually, by searching the word "praxis" through the app WittFind, we observe that the concept of praxis occurs for the first time in Wittgenstein's Dictionary: we find in it two occurrences which are relevant, but they could be considered rather instinctive because they are not the result of real philosophical thinking about the concept of praxis. Them, the word "praxis" appears in Ts-112 of 1931 in the following passage published in *Philosophical Grammar*: "This dispute is similar to the one between realism and idealism! E.g. in the fact that it will very soon have become obsolete & that both parties claim injustices contrary to their daily praxis". Wittgenstein refers here to the ordinary praxis to resolve the fight between formalism and substantial mathematics that is like that between idealism and realism. In that period, Wittgenstein was influenced in his thinking about mathematics by the discussion with Ramsey thanks to which he was developing a pragmatist conception of mathematics. The introduction of the concept of praxis in Wittgenstein's philosophy could be determined by these discussions and so by Ramsey's ideas. As David highlights (2002, p. 138), thanks to the concept of praxis, Wittgenstein uses a way of understanding concepts and ideas based on their placement in a practical context. This way of understanding is like the Marxian method of understanding phenomena used by Sraffa and Gramsci that allows us to clarify important aspects of the concepts and ideas.

Wittgenstein thinks that philosophy should give back to language the real functions that it has in the daily life of people. The understanding of what happens in our private and public life takes form always in a language. We conceptualize the phenomena by language and so we create a critical linguistic space where it is possible to think and re-think them where it emerges that social praxis and language are characterized by an unavoidable twine. It is a Marxian anthropological way of thinking about language for which Wittgenstein declares himself indebted to the Italian economist Piero Sraffa with whom he had engaging discussions from February 1929 to the year before his death with up and down and with an abrupt suspension of two years after 1948 (De Iaco, 2018).

The analogies which we can find between Wittgenstein's new method to do philosophy of language and the Marxian way of thinking are the following:

- The emphasis upon circumstances. There is no meaning of words as well as there is no intrinsic value of commodities without a use of both words and commodities in a certain context.

- The meaning of words as the value of commodities is public. They both could not be private because they come from a public use of them by persons in the shared sphere of the society. They both are the product of an agreement between human beings.

- Commodities and words could be affected by fetishism: they can reflect on the society values assigned by the community of people which used them.

- The reference to models present in Wittgenstein's philosophy is like the use of models by classical economics: Wittgenstein uses language games as models of language uses from simple to more complex which can throw light on the various functions of language and on specific aspects of language functions.

Nevertheless, from a Marxian point of view, we can remark that in Wittgenstein's thought lacks, as for instance Rossi Landi underlines (1966), an historical-social theory. Therefore, although starting from the Thirties, Sraffa's criticism influenced Wittgenstein's way of thinking about language, there are almost two important differences between Wittgenstein's philosophy of language and the Marxist philosophical approach:

- in Wittgenstein's philosophy we find the public dimension of language, but we do not find the historical-social implications of the public character of this dimension. So, the language games that Wittgenstein used in his arguments seem detached from the social context; they appear as something already constituted abstractly beyond any active social-historical process.

- in addiction, also the concept of linguistic use seems to be something already constituted: it is devoid of production; it is not considered as the result of a linguistic labor.

4. *Conclusions*

The highlighted differences depend on the different goals of Wittgenstein's and Marx's or a Marxian philosophy: Wittgenstein's philosophy does not have the purpose to change society through the thought and the rethinking of language. It does not look at the society: it focused on the goal of changing the philosopher's look by converting it towards the everyday language uses despite of the metaphysical ones. Although Wittgenstein focused on the role of praxis in the meaning processes of language, he missed to consider these processes from an historical point of view. As Wittgenstein acknowledged in one of the newly discovered letters to Sraffa of 1934, that of 21 February, Wittgenstein perceived that his thought and that of Sraffa had two different movements (De Iaco, 2019): Sraffa perceived that Wittgenstein did not refer to concrete situations and during the discussions he used to jump from one point of an argument to another in an abstract way without providing effective reasons. Nevertheless, we should assume that Wittgenstein's philosophy gave us the right method to analyse the concrete language uses. We can use this method in a complementary way to the Marxist conceptual tools for investigating the socio-historical processes that affect language and the real life with which language is intertwined.

References

Davis B. J. (2002). A Marxist influence on Wittgenstein via Sraffa. In G. Kitching, N. Pleasants (Eds.) *Marx and Wittgenstein. Knowledge, morality and politics.* New York: Routledge.

Davis B. J. (2010). Gramsci, Sraffa, Wittgenstein: philosophical linkages. *The European Journal of the History of Economic Thought*, vol. 9, no. 3, 2010, pp. 384-401, 2010.

De Iaco M. (2018). A List of Meetings between Wittgenstein and Sraffa. *Nordic Wittgenstein Review*, v. 7, n. 1, pp. 83-99, 2018.

De Iaco M. (2019). Wittgenstein to Sraffa: two newly-discovered letters from February and March 1934. *Nordic Wittgenstein Review*, vol. 8, no. 1-2, pp. 209-223, 2019.

De Iaco M. (2020). *Wittgenstein e Sraffa*. Roma: Aracne.

Gakis D. (2015). Wittgenstein, Marx and Marxism: Some Historical Connections. *Humanities*, Vol. 4, No. 4, pp. 924-937.

Janik A. (1985). Wittgenstein, Marx and Sociology. In *Essays on Wittgenstein and Weininger*. Amsterdam: Rodopi, pp. 136-157.

Kitching G., Pleasants N. (Eds.) (2002). *Marx and Wittgenstein. Knowledge, morality and politics*. New York: Routledge.

Lo Piparo F. (2010). Gramsci and Wittgenstein: an Intriguing Connection. In A. Capone (Ed.), *Perspectives on Language Use and Pragmatics. A volume in Memory of Sorin Stati*. Munich: Lincom Europa Academic Publications, pp. 285-319.

Marjanović A. (2005). Introduzione alla vita e alle carte di Raffaello Piccoli: un racconto. In *Cartevive. Periodico dell'Archivio Prezzolini*, I, Giugno, 2005, pp. 26-84.

Marx K., Engels F. (1998). *The German Ideology*, Prometheus Book, New York.

McGuinness B. (2013). Wittgenstein e Dostoevsky. In A. Ponzio (Ed.). *Figure e forme del narrare. Incontri di prospettive*. Trad. it. a cura di M. De Iaco. Lecce: Milella.

Monk R. (1990). *Ludwig Wittgenstein. The Duty of Genius*. London: Jonathan Cape, London.

Moran H. (1972). Wittgenstein and Russia. *New Left Review*, LXXIII, May-June, 1972.

Nyíri J. C. (1982). Wittgenstein's Later Work in Relation to Conservatism. In B. McGuinness (Ed.), *Wittgenstein and his time*. Chicago: University of Chicago Press, pp. 44-68.

Rhees R. (Ed.). (1984). *Recollections of Wittgenstein: Hermine Wittgenstein--Fania Pascal--F.R. Leavis--John King--M. O'C. Drury*. Oxford: Oxford University Press.

Rossi-Landi F. (1966). Toward a Marxian Use of Wittgenstein. In G. Kitching and N. Pleasants (Eds), *Marx and Wittgenstein; Knowledge, Morality and Politics*. London: Routledge, 2002, pp.185-212.

Rubinstein D. (1981). *Marx and Wittgenstein. Social Praxis and Social Explanation*. London-Boston: Routledge & Kegan Paul.

Sen A. (2003). Sraffa, Wittgenstein and Gramsci. *Journal of Economic Literature*, vol. 41, pp. 1240-1255.

Wittgenstein L. (1958). *Philosophical Investigations*. Oxford: Basil Blackwell.

Wittgenstein L. (2008). *Wittgenstein in Cambridge. Letters and Documents 1911-1951*. Oxford: Blackwell.

2.
LANGUAGE AND MIND

FELICE CIMATTI

MARX, GRAMSCI AND WITTGENSTEIN ON MIND AND LANGUAGE

Dear Sraffa,
I wish to try to formulate what it is that irritates you about the thinking of Cambridge people and of me in particular. Couldn't one say that you feel something of this sort: Here are people who try to speak in a queer way "impartially" about things, they pretend to be able to slip out of their own skins and they speak as though they could understand everybody's feelings, wishes, tendencies etc. It is as though actors forgot that they weren't really all the people they impersonated. – When they talk of the claims of different nations they either try to take up the position of a God, impartial, etc.; or if they take sides they have a theory as well which shows them that their side is the only side, and without this theory they wouldn't dare to take sides (Wittgenstein 2008: 328).

1. On one side the somewhat antiquated and bearded philosopher of *Das Kapital*, on the other side the rich (at least until he gave up his own inheritance) philosopher of family-resemblances. On one side politics and revolution, on the other side language and the mystical. It seems as if there can be no connection at all between those two figures of philosophy (both of which now have in common that they seem quite old-fashioned). However, first occasionally and in the last years more constantly, a growing attention has been devoted to some possible conceptual if not historical commonalities between them (Rubienstein 1981; Janik 1985; Sparti, 2000; Kitching, Pleasants 2013; Lo Piparo 2014; Gakis 2015; 2018; Jost, Hardin 2015; De Iaco 2019). In fact, leaving aside how much Wittgenstein actually read books by Marx (Moran 1972), what they have in common (in the case of the former at least from the so-called 'second' Wittgenstein) is a peculiar social and anthropological perspective from which 'philosophical' problems are addressed, in particular that of language and mind[1]:

---

1   It is well known that it is highly disputable whether an entity such as a genuinely "philosophical problem" can exist according to Marx and Wittgenstein. The last

As far as Wittgenstein's later philosophy is concerned, there are three points on which his philosophical perspective converges with the one of Marx. The first has to do with their shared critique of the phenomenon of reification. The second, with their common conception of language as a matter of social praxis, their shared rejection of the idea of a private language, and their common prioritization of everyday language over metaphysical or philosophical language; and the third, with their shared emphasis on the notion of the 'common' and on the communal aspects of human life and praxis. (Gakis, 2015, p. 935)

While at least from Descartes the starting point of a description of any psychological or social problem was the original *Cogito* – that is an individual entity able to think and speak autonomously – on the contrary Marx (Gramsci) and Wittgenstein place social relations first. At the beginning is not the *Cogito*, on the contrary, at the beginning there is a public intersubjective, or better, presubjective space. Such an approach is now undergoing a widespread diffusion, well beyond 'classical' philosophy: for example, nowadays the main cognitive approach to human cognition is clearly a Marxist-Wittgensteinian one, even if probably nobody is aware of such a noble philosophical descent (Tomasello, 1999; Clark, 2008; Cimatti, 2014; Newen *at al.* 2019).

2. In no sense can one define Marx as a philosopher of language, let alone as a philosopher of mind. The point is that the very existence of separate academic disciplines named "philosophy of language" or "philosophy of mind" is a very recent invention. This is not simply a historiographical observation, on the contrary, at least up to the end of the Second World War nobody believed that "language" or "mind" could exist as autonomous entities. In the history of Western philosophy language, mind and society have never been considered separately. In this sense, one cannot find in Marx a specific philosophy of language. This is exactly the point. If such a

---

of the *Theses on Feuerbach* explicitly says that "the philosophers have only *interpreted* the world, in various ways; the point is to *change* it" (Marx and Engels, 1998, p. 574). Something similar applies to Wittgenstein, who wrote in his *Philosophical Investigations*: "if someone were to advance theses in philosophy, it would never be possible to debate them, because everyone would agree to them" (Wittgenstein, 2009, I, § 128). Notwithstanding their skepticism about the very existence of "philosophical problems", a multitude of philosophers who followed them used their ideas to develop a better comprehension of open questions such as the nature of "mind" and "language". This chapter places itself in this tradition of research, in particular trying to make a constructive use of Wittgenstein despite his ideas about philosophy and philosophical research.

thing as a Marxian philosophy of language exists, one has to search for it scattered in his economic and historical analysis (Holborow 1999; 2006). That is, language is only a constituent of that "complicated form of life" (Wittgenstein 2009, i § 1) that is human life. One cannot understand what language is without taking into account the whole of human life. This is the key character of any possible Marxian philosophy of language and mind (Vološinov 1982; Cook 1982; Lecercle, 2004; Virno, 2003; Sériot, 2011; Jessop, 2017). This approach is at odds with the logical model that Wittgenstein held at the time of the *Tractatus*. While this last approach is radically disembodied, in the Marxian one language is inseparable from the social life of human beings. For example, one cannot take into consideration the human mind without considering the role of language in shaping thought, and the role of social and political life in shaping both. Take the following quote from the first pages of the *Introduction to the Critique of Political Economy* (1859):

> Man is in the most literal sense of the word a *zoon politikon*, not only a social animal, but an animal which can develop into an individual only in society. Production by isolated individuals outside of society—something which might happen as an exception to a civilized man who by accident got into the wilderness and already dynamically possessed within himself the forces of society— is as great an absurdity as the idea of the development of language without individuals living together and talking to one another. (Marx and Engels, 1998, p. 2)

This is a point of much interest for a Wittgensteinian ear. To be a *zoon politikon* does not mean that a human being exists first, and that such a being can then eventually participate in social-political life, as if the social dimension of human life were important but not necessary. Quite the contrary, it means that a human animal can be said human exactly because it is literally constituted by social relations (Cimatti, 2000; 2017). A human being is *human* because society is deep inside her. The Marxist psychologist Vygosky expresses this point with a radical formulation: "the great fundamental law of psychology [...]. The collective origin of the higher psychological functions. About their twofold appearance on the scene in the process of the development of the higher functions: as inter- and intrapsychological categories" (Vygotsky, 2018, p. 156). Those which in the mind of an adult are 'her' cognitive processes once were social relations among different persons. Take the case of the capacity to explicitly reason about some practical problem. In this case, the main obstacle for an *infans* mind is its difficulty to maintain the concentration on the same object for more than a few seconds. On the contrary, in an interpersonal situation a mother – for example with her focused linguistic comments – helps an *infans* not to distract itself. In this case, the attention of the *infants* is mediated by the verbal discourse of another human being. That is, properly speaking, the *infants* 'thinks' inside a mind that is different from its own. Its own thought is outside its own mind. The dramatic step in the cognitive development of the mind of an *infans* shows itself when it becomes able to 'reproduce' the previous interpersonal situation inside 'its' mind. At this point, such a process becomes an intrapsychological process, that is, a process that develops inside the mind of the *infans*. In fact, such a mind is nothing other than the capacity to internally reactivate external social relations. The most elaborate form of this intrapsychological cognitive process is so-called "verbal thinking", that is, the 'internal' flow of consciousness that is literally made up of internalized social (that is, external) discourses:

> All (verbal) thinking of cultural man is a system of external speech mechanisms ingrown in consciousness [...]. Language is a mnemotechnic tool; memorizing the verbal (the verbal type of memory). [...] Preverbal thinking and pre-intellectual speech is the first stage. *Before* the moment they meet [...] the inability to think with the help of speech — the second stage (to a certain extent until 14 yrs. — before the abstract concepts). *Naïve Psychologie*. The moment they meet — the third stage, the instrumental method [...] (perhaps the shortest stage). Verbal thinking — the fourth stage, when the external mechanisms (speech) become internal (intel[lectualized]). The advantage of speech for thinking is that (1) in making thinking an external activity, it makes it possible to master thinking, and (2) *most importantly*, by creating external mechanisms subordinated to the will, it makes them grow into consciousness and converts them into internal mechanisms. Man masters himself from the outside and changes his whole inner world. [...] The fourth stage is the *environment in us*, culture that has been absorbed, language that has become thinking, history within psychology. (*Ibid.*, pp.118-119)

One can consider this description of the human cognitive development as an articulated paraphrase of the preceding observation by Marx. To be a *zoon politikon* literally means that society is inside the mind, that is, that the human mind is an intrinsically social mind. This is the point that radically separates this cognitive perspective from the Cartesian one. According to the latter at the beginning there is an individual mind; according the former there are social relations. The first approach is somewhat ahistorical and disembodied, as one can see in the *Tractatus*. On the contrary, the second is radically embodied in a specific cultural tradition and in a specific language.

In these two perspectives, the role of language is very different; in the Cartesian perspective language is nothing other than a communicative device, which carries outside the internal and private thoughts. In the second perspective, language is the bodily substance of thinking, as Marx and Engels wrote in the *German Ideology*:

> Man [...] possesses "consciousness". But even from the outset this is not "pure" consciousness. The "mind" is from the outset afflicted with the curse of being "burdened" with matter, which here makes its appearance in the form of agitated layers of air, sounds, in short, of language. Language is as old as consciousness, language is practical, real consciousness that exists for other men as well, and only therefore does it also exist for me; language, like consciousness, only arises from the need, the necessity of intercourse with other men. [...] Consciousness is, therefore, from the very beginning a social product. (Marx and Engels, 1998, pp. 49-50)

There is no such a thing as pure 'logical' thinking. From the very beginning, thinking is permeated by the fleshy materiality of language, that is, by the verbal sounds (or by gestures in the case of the language of signs). Language and (self)consciousness are nothing other than two sides of a same socio-historical cognitive process. This means that since language is a social process – in fact it is the prototype of any social process – the so-called private internal thinking is in principle completely public. There is nothing private in the mind. Obviously one can be silent; however, such a silence does not stop being a social action like any other social action. One must not confuse silence with a psychological private event. One can indeed be silent only because one can speak openly. All language-games involve the presence of silence as a legitimate *linguistic* move. A tree is not silent, because it cannot speak. Therefore, either language is social or it is not language. Consequently, there cannot be such a thing as 'private' – that is, radically alien in respect to sociality – thinking:

> Far from it being true that "out of nothing" I make myself, for example, a "speaker", the nothing which forms the basis here is a very manifold something, the real individual, his speech organs, a definite stage of physical development, an existing language and dialects, ears capable of hearing and a human environment from which it is possible to hear something, etc. (*ibid.*, p.162)

This a completely Anti-Cartesian presupposition. Nobody begins thinking by herself, "out of nothing". There is a communism of ideas before the communism of properties (Cimatti, 2011). The point is that language and thinking are two sides of one single entity. There is no thinking on one side and language on the other; uniquely human cognitive processes are those processes where language and thinking are inextricably interlaced. Language is intrinsically social, therefore thinking is social too: "*language is the immediate actuality of thought*" (*ibid.*, p. 482). Marx absolutely excludes the possibility of such a thing as an isolated human being, that is, not someone who is alone (loneliness is a social possibility), but someone who becomes fully human apart from human relations. This is a crucial point if one wants to establish a sound relationship between Marx and Wittgenstein. In fact, from the social nature of language it derives that the individual mind is also a social entity. As Marx wrote in the first page of the *Introduction to the Critique of Political Economy*, the myth of an original autonomous human being it is only a Robinsonade, that is a literary phantasy:

> The subject of our discussion is first of all material production by individuals as determined by society, naturally constitutes the starting point. The individual and isolated hunter or fisher who forms the starting point with Smith and Ricardo, belongs to the insipid illusions of the eighteenth century. They are Robinsonades which do not by any means represent, as students of the history of civilization imagine, a reaction against over-refinement and a return to a misunderstood natural life. They are no more based on such a naturalism than is Rousseau's "contract social", which makes naturally independent individuals come in contact and have mutual intercourse by contract. They are the fiction and only the aesthetic fiction of the small and great Robinsonades. (Marx and Engels, 1998, p. 1)

3. Perhaps the first to identify the hidden similarities between Marx and Wittgenstein was the Italian philosopher Ferruccio Rossi-Landi (1921-1985) in a seminal paper written in 1966, "Per un uso marxiano di Wittgenstein" (*Towards a Marxian use of Wittgenstein*)[2]. This paper was written at a time when at least in Italy the dominant philosophical tradition was Marxism, and when Wittgenstein was still little known in continental Europe. It is an important paper because it is still useful today to identify – at least from a theoretical point of view, even if perhaps not yet historically – the concepts where Marx and Wittgenstein meet. I will draw on such a paper because it explicitly addresses many of the points in which the 'influence' that Marx had on Wittgenstein seems more evident.

---

2   The quotations from this paper come from the partial English translation published in Kitching, Pleasants eds., 2013, pp. 185-212.

Rossi-Landi's philosophical hypothesis is that the key difference between the *Tractatus* and *Philosophische Untersuchungen*is is that in the last book one can find "the flow of life" (Rossi-Landi, 2013, p. 192) which is completely absent in the first one. What is at stake is the source of such a flow. According to Rossi-Landi the key figure in such a passage is the economist Sraffa, who mediated between him and Gramsci: "individuals are bearers of intellectual traditions, and it is their contact with one another as such bearers that produces revolutionary changes in ideas. Thus Sraffa's displacement from Italy to Britain [...] brought two histories of ideas into proximity with one another that had previously been largely separate" (Davis, 2013, p. 141). The two traditions that Sraffa brought into proximity were the British logical and aseptic one at the origin of *Tractatus* and the socio-historical tradition of Marx. Through such an encounter Wittgenstein realized the "a private language [...] is a contradiction in terms" (Rossi-Landi, 2013, p. 202). A theory of language which is not part of a more ample theory of social relations cannot work. The idea is that Marx brings Wittgenstein into an anthropological vision of language: "there is a sense in which Karl Marx and Ludwig Wittgenstein may even appear complementary or, in certain aspects, actually at one" (*ibid.*, p. 210). What both have in common is the method of paying attention mainly "to the real circumstances in which things—including the particular 'things' that constitute language—gain their meaning. Outside a real context, things have no meaning, or lend themselves to being assimilated and debased within preconceived schemata to which they do not belong" (*ibid.*, p. 201). In order to understand what this really implies we may take the case of the notion of 'proposition' Wittgenstein develops in the *Tractatus*: "A proposition is a picture of reality. A proposition is a model of reality as we imagine it" (Wittgenstein, 1961, § 4.01). What makes a proposition meaningful is the fact of being a logical image of reality. The meaningful capacity of a proposition is 'inside' such a proposition, in its own logical character. At the same time "a logical picture of facts is a thought" (§ 3), and "a thought is a proposition with a sense" (§ 4). That is, thinking is a peculiar logical-linguistic activity, which takes place in such a strange entity to whom Wittgenstein refuses any actual existence: in fact "there is no such thing as the [...] subject" (§ 5.5421). The subject cannot exist because it does not play any role in the logical machinery of language and thought. If one strictly adheres to Wittgenstein's definitions in the *Tractatus* there is language but there are no speakers of such a language. There is logic but no human life.

With respect to such an 'ethereal' position, the *Philosophical Investigations* represent a dramatic change. Now the value of human activities is not mainly logical nor cognitive; as Rossi-Landi wrote, in this book one can see a shift toward "the contextual and real situations in which words take on meaning (more precisely: in which they *become* words) further back to the communal existence of men, who are the actors-out of meaning. Not merely to a biological, but to a public communal life, compared to which the private experiences of the subjects are revealed to be secondary" (Rossi-Landi, 2013, p. 202). While in the *Tractatus* at the beginning there was logic, now there are very specific "language-games", where each "language-game is used here to emphasize the fact that the speaking of language is part of an activity, or of a form of life" (Wittgenstein 2009, I § 23). Life and history enter into language and thought. This is a point which deserves some comment, because Rossi-Landi instead thought that Wittgenstein missed the peculiar social-historical dimension of human life: "the idea Wittgenstein never seems to have grasped, or at least not grasped as fundamental, is that individuals have socially formed themselves as individuals precisely because, among other things, *they have begun* to talk to one another" (Rossi-Landi, 2013, p. 208). In fact, Wittgenstein points out on the part of the *infans* that the passage from a somewhat 'natural' ('animal') condition to a human one is nothing but an effect of first being captured in the linguistic-games, and secondly of mastering the capacity to follow the social rules of these game. Take the case of the proposition where Wittgenstein describes the situation by which a little child learns to participate in the "language-game" of expressing pain of its own language-culture. In fact in this situation, the child does not only learn how to express pain, she actually learns how to *feel* pain in a human way:

> How do words *refer* to sensations? – There doesn't seem to be any problem here; don't we talk about sensations every day, and name them? But how is the connection between the name and the thing named set up? This question is the same as: How does a human being learn the meaning of names of sensations? For example, of the word "pain". Here is one possibility: words are connected with the primitive, natural, expressions of sensation and used in their place. A child has hurt himself and he cries; then adults talk to him and teach him exclamations and, later, sentences. They teach the child new pain-behaviour. "So you are saying that the word 'pain' really means crying?" – On the contrary: the verbal expression of pain replaces crying, it does not describe it. (Wittgenstein, 2009, I, § 244)

Take the case of an Italian child learning to use the linguistic expression "Che male!" (That hurts!), an expression used when someone feels a strong pain in some part of the body. A naïve description of this situation would be the following one: there is first (phylogenetically and ontogenetically) a 'primitive' expression of pain, which is then substituted by the cultural and learned expression "Che male!". The point made by Wittgenstein is much more complex, because "the verbal expression of pain replaces crying, it does not describe it". That is, "Che male!" is not a simple synonymous of the presumed primitive expression of pain. On the contrary, learning to use the verbal expression "Che male!" implies learning a completely new behavior of pain. This means that prelinguistic pain is different from such a pain, which is included in the language-game of "pain". One can say that in the first case the child and pain are indistinguishable (the child *is* pain), while in the second case the child *has* pain. Now the child has at her own disposal the feeling that she actually feels: for example, she can ask for help to relieve the pain. Such a passage is exactly the passage from nature to culture/history. From this point of view, at least implicitly, Wittgenstein is adopting an historical-anthropological perspective: "What we are supplying are really remarks on the natural history of human beings" (Wittgenstein, 2009, I, § 415). Therefore, it is not completely correct, as Rossi-Landi wrote, that "this *taking place in public is not, however, seen as existing socially*" (Rossi-Landi, 2013, p. 207). In fact the situation described in the § 244 the first part of *Philosophical Investigations* is not generically public, it is a specific social situation where an *infans* acquires the competence to participate in a special language-game. Such a language-game is specific of a determinate society, that is, of a determinate culture.

In the passage from the *Tractatus* to the *Philosophical Investigations* Wittgenstein does not only abandon a logical and metahistorical vision of language, in fact he proposes an ontogenetic perspective on language. In the *Tractatus* it would have been incorrect to claim that to speak a language implies a 'mental' capacity. In fact language, as logic, transcendentally precedes the capacity to speak it: "man possesses the ability to construct languages capable of expressing every sense, without having any idea how each word has meaning or what its meaning is—just as people speak without knowing how the individual sounds are produced. Everyday language is a part of the human organism and is no less complicated than it" (Wittgenstein, 1961, § 4.002). On the contrary, in the *Philosophical Investigations* any definitional question about the 'nature' of language is dismissed in favor of an inquiry into the way human beings learn to participate in a particular language-game. In this sense, one can read numerous propositions of this book as an anthropological description of the peculiar behaviors of the animal species *Homo sapiens*. Therefore, to speak a language is no longer a logical experience, it is a kind of social activity.

This point allows to respond to another critique that Rossi-Landi moves against Wittgenstein. According to Rossi-Landi what is at stake is the presumed scarce attention that Wittgenstein attributes to the historical-evolutionary dimension of language: "even the child who learns a new word and uses it for the first time is exercising this behaviour of his on something that has preceded him (and that will therefore compel him to 'see a piece of the world' in a certain way). But how was this word originally produced?" (Rossi-Landi, 2013, p. 208). In fact, Wittgenstein addresses such a problem in many places of the *Philosophical Investigations*. Take the case of a very simple language-game described in § 2, that takes place between a builder and his assistant (it is not that different from many cases of non-human animal communication systems; Hauser, 1999):

> Let us imagine a language [...] [that] is meant to serve for communication between a builder A and an assistant B. A is building with building stones: there are blocks, pillars, slabs and beams. B has to pass him the stones and to do so in the order in which A needs them. For this purpose they make use of a language consisting of the words "block", "pillar", "slab", "beam". A calls them out; B brings the stone which he has learnt to bring at such-and-such a call. —— Conceive of this as a complete primitive language. (Wittgenstein, 2009, § 2)

In this case, the "meaning" of the words of this simple language-game is nothing but what the participants *do* with them. That is, meaning is no more a private 'mental' entity, quite the contrary: "if we had to name anything which is the life of the sign, we should have to say that it was its *use*" (Wittgenstein, 1969, p. 4). The shift from meaning to use it is an effect of the "flow of life" that for Rossi-Landi characterizes the so-called second Wittgenstein. A life, which is made of human uses and actions with words, that is, language-games. It is in this context that the question of learning becomes relevant. Since language is not mainly a logical capacity but a form of action, the problem that arises concerns how one can acquire such a capacity: "a child uses such primitive forms of language when he learns to talk. Here the teaching of language is not explaining, but training" (Wittgenstein, 2009, § 5). Training means a social and normative situation where someone who still does not possess a certain capacity is trained to behave in a specific way. This means that from this moment on the most important character of language is its intrinsic sociality: "following a rule competently depends upon seeing how that rule functions in its language-game, within the form of life in which it is embedded. This is fundamentally a *practical* rather than an *intellectual* (interpretive) task" (Davis, 2013, p. 138).

4. In this vein, the 'second' Wittgenstein's most important concept is the critique of private language. The hypothesis of this chapter is that such a critique represents the core of the *Philosophical Investigations*. As the previous analysis of Marx has shown, it is around the impossibility of a private language that one can find the more extended conceptual similarity between Marx (through Gramsci-Sraffa) and Wittgenstein. A conceptual similarity that probably derives from a more or less verified historical connection[3]. Let's read the famous proposition of the *Philosophical Investigations* where Wittgenstein develops his clear critique of the possibility that such a thing as private language may exist:

> Let's imagine the following case. I want to keep a diary about the recurrence of a certain sensation. To this end I associate it with the sign "S" and write this sign in a calendar for every day on which I have the sensation. —— I first want to observe that a definition of the sign cannot be formulated. – But all the same, I can give one to myself as a kind of ostensive definition! – How? Can I point to the sensation? – Not in the ordinary sense. But I speak, or write the sign down, and at the same time I concentrate my attention on the sensation – and so, as it were, point to it inwardly. – But what is this ceremony for? For that is all it seems to be! A definition serves to lay down the meaning of a sign, doesn't it? – Well, that is done precisely by concentrating my attention; for in this way I commit to memory the connection between the sign and the sensation. – But "I commit it to memory" can only mean: this process brings it about that I remember the connection correctly in the future. But in the present case, I have no criterion of correctness. One would like to say: whatever is going to seem correct to me is correct. And that only means that here we can't talk about 'correct'. (Wittgenstein, 2009, I § 258)

---

3   Since the seminal papers of Davis (2002) and Sen (2003), the relationship of Wittgenstein to Marx, through the mediation of Sraffa and Gramsci, has received much attention (Sinha, 2009; Venturinha, 2011; Schweizer, 2012; Cospito, 2016). For example, in *Il professor Gramsci e Wittgenstein* Franco Lo Piparo (2014) reconstructs in much detail the possible historical influences that Gramsci (and through him Marx) could have had (precisely through the mediation of Sraffa) on Wittgenstein. For example, Lo Piparo acutely observes that the sudden and unexpected (it is a term never used before by him) appearance of the Marxist term "praxis" in the *Philosophische Untersuchungen* – as when he writes of "Praxis der Sprache" (Wittgenstein, 2009, I § 51) – could be an element of textual proof of such a mediated relationship (Lo Piparo, 2014, p. 75).

If such a thing as "private language" could exist, it would not be a language at all. In fact, the same maker of this language would not be able to use it legitimately. A use is legitimate when the possibility exists to distinguish between a correct and an incorrect use of a linguistic expression. The point is that such a possibility is excluded in principle when there is only one speaker for a language. A lonely speaker cannot discriminate between a correct or incorrect use, because in both cases there is no external 'authority' – a grammar – that establishes what is correct and what it is not correct. In any case, the lonely speaker can only *believe* that his use is correct. Nevertheless, this only means that there is "no criterion of correctness". A private language does not exist because a private grammar cannot exist. Without a social grammar there is no language. Grammar is intrinsically social and a private language is without grammar, therefore such a language cannot exist. It is worth noting that in the *Tractatus* Wittgenstein only speaks of "logical grammar" as "logical syntax" (Wittgenstein, 1969, § 3.325).

The question now arises regarding how to explain such a radical passage from a "logical grammar" to the very different idea of grammar of the *Philosophical Investigations*: "grammar does not tell us how language must be constructed in order to fulfil its purpose, in order to have such-and-such an effect on human beings. It only describes, and in no way explains, the use of signs" (Wittgenstein, 2009, I § 496). Grammar has become a descriptive social human entity, while logic has lost the power – the *Tractatus* was constructed around such a power – to dictate how to use language to human beings. It is no surprise that, with reference to the mention of the possible existing links between Gramsci and Wittgenstein, in 1935 the last *Prison Notebook* (n. 29, *Note per una introduzione allo studio della grammatica*; Lo Piparo, 1979; Carlucci, 2013) Gramsci explicitly writes that "la grammatica è 'storia'" ("grammar is history"; Gramsci 2001, p. 2341). This assertion contains an idea of language as a historical stratified entity, an idea that we will find in the *Philosophical Investigations*. In the *Notebook* n. 11 (1932-1933), Gramsci explicitly criticizes the idea that language has to be corrected because it is too metaphoric and imprecise.

In fact, Gramsci is criticizing Wittgenstein's idea of language as presented in the *Tractatus*, where he claimed that "the configuration of objects in a situation corresponds to the configuration of simple signs in the propositional sign" (Wittgenstein 1961, § 3.21). In such a logical and strictly referential view of language there is no space for metaphor. "Language", however, "is always metaphorical. If perhaps it cannot quite be said that all discourse is metaphorical in respect of the thing or material and sensible object referred to (or the abstract concept) [...], it can however be said that present language is metaphorical with respect to the meanings and the ideological content which the words used had in preceding periods of civilization" (Gramsci, 1971, p. 450). What is at stake is the very nature of language. In the *Tractatus* Wittgenstein held that the main if not unique function of language was to describe the world truthfully. On the contrary, Gramsci points out that language is made of a multitude of social and functional strata. There is no such a thing as *the* language:

> The pragmatists theorise abstractly about language as a source of error [...]. But is it possible to remove from language its metaphorical and extensive meanings? It is not possible. Language is transformed with the transformation of the whole of civilisation, through the acquisition of culture by new classes and through the hegemony exercised by one national language over others, etc., and what it does is precisely to absorb in metaphorical form the words of previous civilisations and cultures. Nobody today thinks that the word "disaster" is connected with astrology or can claim to be misled about the opinions of someone who uses the word. Similarly even an atheist can speak of "dis-grace" without being thought to be a believer in predestination (etc.). The new "metaphorical" meaning spreads with the spread of the new culture, which furthermore also coins brand-new words or absorbs them from other languages as loan-words giving them a precise meaning and therefore depriving them of the extensive halo they possessed in the original language. (*Ibid.*, pp. 451-452)

Language does not exist as a single self-sufficient logical apparatus. The life of language is the life of human beings who use language in their lives. In this sense language is a historical entity that changes in time and that has many different uses. It is not surprising to find a similar idea in the *Philosophical Investigations*, where Wittgenstein compares language to an ancient town: "our language can be regarded as an ancient city: a maze of little streets and squares, of old and new houses, of houses with extensions from various periods, and all this surrounded by a multitude of new suburbs with straight and regular streets and uniform houses" (Wittgenstein, 2009, I § 18). Now language is "our" language, the language of human beings. A language that contains modern and well-planned districts (the scientific languages), old and obscure streets (the daily language of simple life), parks and ancient monuments (the aesthetics use of language).

But how many kinds of sentence are there? Say assertion, question and command? –There are countless kinds; countless different kinds of use of all the things we call "signs", "words", "sentences". And this diversity is not something fixed, given once for all; but new types of language, new language-games, as we may say, come into existence, and others become obsolete and get forgotten. [...]

Consider the variety of language-games in the following examples, and in others:

Giving orders, and acting on them –

Describing an object by its appearance, or by its measurements –

Constructing an object from a description (a drawing) –

Reporting an event –

Speculating about the event –

Forming and testing a hypothesis –

Presenting the results of an experiment in tables and diagrams –

Making up a story; and reading one –

Acting in a play –

Singing rounds –

Guessing riddles –

Cracking a joke; telling one –

Solving a problem in applied arithmetic –

Translating from one language into another –

Requesting, thanking, cursing, greeting, praying.

– It is interesting to compare the diversity of the tools of language and of the ways they are used, the diversity of kinds of word and sentence, with what logicians have said about the structure of language. (This includes the author of the *Tractatus Logico-Philosophicus*.). (*Ibid.*, § 23)

5. In the *Blue Book* Wittgenstein says that "we shall also try to construct new notations, in order to break the spell of those which we are accustomed to" (Wittgenstein, 1969, p. 23). Pietro Sraffa, in a short comment on his own copy of this book, writes the following observation: "but why should we want to?" (reported in Venturinha, 2012, p. 185). This is a question the *Tractatus* cannot answer. In fact, the gelid logical apparatus of this book does not foresee any space for change. The point is that there is no change because in that book there is no life. However, the simple presence of human life is not sufficient to introduce the possibility of change in the logical world of the *Tractatus*. To make space for the possibility (and necessity) of such a change Wittgenstein had to introduce in his own vision of language a political point of view, one he had not been favourably disposed towards previously. It is not difficult to identify a possible source of this new disposition in the pages of the *Notebooks* n. 11 where Gramsci discusses the critical character of the "philosophy of praxis". In fact, such a philosophy explicitly aims to

change the way human beings think of their own existence. The idea is that the somewhat unexpected 'ethical-political' character of the *Philosophical Investigations* could be an effect of the discussions with Sraffa, and through him with Gramsci.

The basic point is that according to Marx and Gramsci the actual life of human beings is determined by the social structure to whom they largely unconsciously belong. Any possibility to change this situation requires to change this implicit way of thinking, that is, to question the social relations that are sedimented in 'our' thoughts. In particular, those thoughts are crystallized in the 'normal' and unquestioned use of language. Therefore, a critical work on language is required in order to render the idea of change possible. It is important to note that this perspective does not hold that daily language is somewhat erroneous and requires some form of logical amendment. The point is that the first thing anyone has to do is a critical work on what is unconsciously *supposed* in one's own thoughts. For this reason according to Gramsci: "it is essential to destroy the widespread prejudice that philosophy is a strange and difficult thing just because it is the specific intellectual activity of a particular category of specialists or of professional and systematic philosophers. It must first be shown that all men are 'philosophers', by defining the limits and characteristics of the 'spontaneous philosophy' which is proper to everybody" (Gramsci, 1971, p. 323). Wittgenstein is no longer the lonely and super-human philosopher who puts the imperfections of daily language in order from an external point of view. Everyone is the bearer of a "spontaneous philosophy" that one is largely unaware of:

> Having first shown that everyone is a philosopher, though in his own way and unconsciously, since even in the slightest manifestation of any intellectual activity whatever, in "language", there is contained a specific conception of the world, one then moves on to the second level, which is that of awareness and criticism. That is to say, one proceeds to the question-is it better to "think", without having a critical awareness, in a disjointed and episodic way? In other words, is it better to take part in a conception of the world mechanically imposed by the external environment, i.e. by one of the many social groups in which everyone is automatically involved from the moment of his entry into the conscious world (and this can be one's village or province [...] Or, on the other hand, is it better to work out consciously and critically one's own conception of the world and thus, in connection with the labours of one's own brain, choose one's sphere of activity, take an active part in the creation of the history of the world, be one's own guide, refusing to accept passively and supinely from outside the moulding of one's personality? (*Ibid.*, pp. 323-324)

One can find a very similar idea in a note written by Wittgenstein in those years (14.10.1931), where in fact he holds that "work on philosophy [...] is really more work on oneself. On one's own conception. On how one sees things. (And what one expects of them.)" (Wittgenstein, 1998, p. 24). Now philosophy is no more a logical and technical activity, it is rather an ethical-political one. In fact, the possibility of a radical change in the economic organization of society is only possible when one realizes that first such a change must happen inside the individual mind: "since all action is political, can one not say that the real philosophy of each man is contained in its entirety in his political action?" (Gramsci, 1971, p. 326). It remains a last and radical question to address, that posed by Sraffa to Wittgenstein, "but why should we want to?" change our language? To answer such a question one has to adopt a completely different perspective in respect to language and mind. The answer does not lie in the individual mind; moreover, it lies in the contradictions between preexisting social-economic relations and the new ones that cannot fit into the former. Thoughts always come to mind from the outside[4]:

> Incidentally, it is quite immaterial what consciousness starts to do on its own: out of all this trash we get only the one inference that these three moments, the productive forces, the state of society and consciousness, can and must come into contradiction with one another, because the division of labour implies the possibility, nay the fact, that intellectual and material activity, that enjoyment and labour, production and consumption, devolve on different individuals, and that the only possibility of their not coming into contradiction lies in negating in its turn the division of labour. (Marx and Engels, 1998, p. 52)

6. The shift from the *Tractatus* to the *Philosophical Investigations*, as Rossi-Landi first noted, is the shift from logic to human life. There is much proof that such a passage could have been prompted by several encounters with Marx and the Marxist tradition (Sraffa, Gramsci). At the core of this vision there is the basic tenet that "in historical materialism thought cannot be separated from being, man from nature, activity (history) from matter, subject from object: such a separation would be a fall into empty talk, meaningless abstraction" (Gramsci, 1996, p. 190).

---

4   It is as if Wittgenstein now would realize that what he wrote in *Tractatus*–"in order to be able to represent logical form, we should have to be able to station ourselves with propositions somewhere outside logic, that is to say outside the world" (Wittgenstein, 1961, § 4.12)–it is not a logical impossibility but only a *practical* one.

References

Carlucci A. (2013). *Gramsci and Languages. Unification, Diversity*, Hegemony. Leiden: Brill.

Cimatti F. (2000). *La scimmia che si parla. Linguaggio, autocoscienza e libertà nell'animale umano*. Torino: Bollati Boringhieri.

Cimatti F. (2011). *Comunismo e natura umana*. Milano: Bruno Mondadori.

Cimatti F. (2014). "L'individuo è essere sociale". Marx e Vygotskij sul transindividuale. In E. Balibar and V. Morfino (Eds.), *Il transindividuale. Soggetti, relazioni, mutazioni*. Milano: Mimesis, pp. 253-271.

Cimatti F. (2017). Cervello e storia. Attualità della psicologia marxista. In P. Garofalo e M. Quante (Eds.), *Lo spettro è tornato! Attualità della filosofia di Marx*. Milano: Mimesis, pp. 39-50.

Clark A. (2008). *Supersizing the Mind: Embodiment, Action, and Cognitive Extension*. Oxford: Oxford University Press.

Cook D. (1982). Marx's Critique of Philosophical Language. *Philosophy and Phenomenological Research*, 42, pp. 530-554.

Cospito G. (Ed.). (2016). *Sraffa e Wittgenstein a Cambridge*. Pisa: Edizioni della Normale di Pisa.

Davis J. (2002). Gramsci, Sraffa, Wittgenstein: Philosophical Linkages. *European Journal of the History of Economic Thought*, 9(3), pp. 384-401.

Davis J. (2013). A Marxist influence on Wittgenstein via Sraffa. In G. Kitching and N. Pleasants (Eds.). (2002), pp. 131-143.

De Iaco M. (2019). "L'alienazione linguistica: Rossi-Landi lettore di Wittgenstein". *Filosofi(e)Semiotiche*, 6(2), pp. 33-39.

Gakis D. (2015). "Wittgenstein, Marx, and Marxism: Some Historical Connections". *Humanities*, 4(4), pp. 924-937.

Gakis D. (2018). The Political Import of Wittgenstein's Philosophical Investigations. *Philosophy and Social Criticism*, 44(3). pp. 229–252.

Gramsci A. (1971). *Selection from the Prison Notebooks*, ed. by Q. Hoare and G. N. Smith. New York: International Publisher.

Gramsci A. (1996). *Prison Notebooks. II*. New York: Columbia University Press.

Gramsci A. (2001). *Quaderni dal carcere*, ed. by V. Gerratana. Torino: Einaudi.

Hauser M. (1999). *The Design of Animal Communication*. Cambridge: The MIT Press.

Holborow M. (1999). *The Politics of English: A Marxist View of Language*. London: Sage.

Holborow M. (2006). Putting the social back into language: Marx, Vološinov and Vygotsky reexamined. In *Studies in language & capitalism*, 1, pp. 1-28.

Kitching G. and Pleasants N. (Eds). (2013). *Marx and Wittgenstein. Knowledge, Morality and Politics*. London: Routledge.

Janik A. (1985). Wittgenstein, Marx and Sociology. In Id. *Essays on Wittgenstein and Weininger*. Amsterdam: Rodopi pp. 136–157.

Jessop B. (2017). From Karl Marx to Antonio Gramsci and Louis Althusser. In R. Wodak, B. Forchtner (Eds.). *The Routledge Handbook of Language and Politics*. London: Routledge pp. 30-42.

Jost J. T., Hardin C. (2015). The practical turn in psychology: Marx and Wittgenstein as social materialists. In I. Parker (Ed.). *Critical Discursive Psychology*. London: Palgrave Macmillan pp. 114-121.

Ives P. (2004). *Gramsci's Political Language: Engaging the Bakhtin Circle & the Frankfurt School*. Toronto: University of Toronto Press.

Lecercle J. J. (2004). *Une philosophie marxiste du langage*. Paris: PUF.

Lo Piparo F. (1979). *Lingua, intellettuali, egemonia in Gramsci*. Bari-Roma: Laterza.

Lo Piparo F. (2014). *Il professor Gramsci e Wittgenstein*. Roma: Donzelli.

Marx K. (1992). *Capital. Critique of Political Economy*. London: Penguin.

Marx K. and Engels F. (1998). *The German Ideology*, including Theses on Feuerbach and Introduction to the Critique of Political Economy. New York: Prometheus Books.

Moran J. (1972). Wittgenstein and Russia. *New Left Review*, 73, pp. 85–96.

Newen A., De Bruin L. and Gallagher S. (Eds.). (2018). *The Oxford Handbook of 4E Cognition*. Oxford: Oxford University Press.

Rossi-Landi F. (1966). Toward a Marxian Use of Wittgenstein. In G. Kitching and N. Pleasants (Eds), *Marx and Wittgenstein; Knowledge, Morality and Politics*. London: Routledge, 2002, pp.185-212.

Rubinstein D. (1981). *Marx and Wittgenstein. Social Praxis and Social Explanation*. London: Routledge & Kegan Paul.

Schweizer M. (2012). *Ricerche su inediti relativi al rapporto Sraffa-Wittgenstein*. Milano: Mimesis.

Sen A. (2003). Sraffa, Wittgenstein and Gramsci. *Journal of Economic Literature*, 41, pp. 1240-1255.

Sériot P. (2011). Vološinov, la philosophie du langage et le marxisme. *Langages*, 2, pp. 83-96.

Sinha A. (2009). Sraffa and the later Wittgenstein. *Contributions to Political Economy*, 28(1), pp. 47-69.

Sparti D. (Ed.) (2000). *Wittgenstein politico*. Milano: Feltrinelli.

Tomasello M. (1999). *The Cultural Origins of Human Cognition.* Cambridge: Harvard University Press.

Virno P. (2003) *Quando il verbo si fa carne. Linguaggio e natura umana.* Torino: Bollati Boringhieri.

Venturinha N. (2011). Wittgenstein's Debt to Sraffa. In J. Padilla Gálvez, M. Gaffal (Eds.). *Forms of Life and Language Games.* Frankfurt: Ontos Verlag, pp. 187-194.

Venturinha N. (2012). "Sraffa's Notes on Wittgenstein's *Blue Book*". *Nordic Wittgenstein Review*, 1, pp. 181-191.

Vološinov V. (1982). *Marxism and the Philosophy of Language.* Cambridge: Harvard University Press.

Vygotsky L. (2018). *Vygotsky's Notebooks. A Selection*, Ekaterina Zavershneva, René van der Veer (eds.). Singapore: Springer.

Wittgenstein L. (1961). *Tractatus Logico-Philosophicus.* London: Routledge.

Wittgenstein L. (1969). *Blue and Brown Books.* Oxford: Blackwell.

Wittgenstein L. (1998). *Culture and Value. A Selection from Posthumous Remains.* Oxford: Blackwell.

Wittgenstein L. (2008). *Wittgenstein in Cambridge. Letters and Documents 1911–1951.* Oxford: Blackwell.

Wittgenstein L. (2009). *Philosophical Investigations.* Oxford: Blackwell.

Pietro Garofalo

CRITIQUE OF LANGUAGE AND CRITIQUE OF HUMAN FORMS OF SOCIAL LIFE IN MARX

1. *Introduction*

Even if Marx did not develop a genuine and systematic conception of language in his writings, we can still find different suggestions of it. For this reason, different philosophers of language, such as Rossi-Landi, Lev Vygotsky, Vološinov and Bachtin have been influenced by Marx' and Engels' writings in the elaboration of their own thought.

However, these authors do not only represent a rare exception, but have also developed their own, very original and autonomous philosophies with results far different from Marx's conception. Vološinov, as noted by Seriot, has never directly mentioned Marx or referred to Marx's quotations in his "Marxism and philosophy of language" (Seriot, 2011, p.86), whereas Rossi-Landi has used Marx's analysis of commodities for his analysis of human communication, achieving results that are not only far from Marx's general conception, but also, in certain aspects are in opposition to it (See Fineschi, 2017; Isreael, 2002, pp.220-224: Newmeyer, 1977).

In recent decades, a very important contribution to Marx's studies in relation to the philosophy of language has been supported by the comparison between Karl Marx and the Austrian philosopher Ludwig Wittgenstein, despite the latter belonging to a radically different tradition. As many scholars have noted, there are not only historical connections between these two authors (Rossi-Landi, 1966; LoPiparo, 2010; Sen, 2003; Gakis, 2015; De Iaco, 2019), but also different theoretical affinities between these two philosophers may be found (Rubinstein, 1981; Kitching and Pleasants, 2002).

This contribution focuses more on discussing certain aspects of Marx's thought by using some of Wittgenstein ideas, rather than proposing a comparison to Wittgenstein. I will try to underline how Marx's critique of the previous philosophies and ideologists corresponds to the critique of certain incorrect uses of language, which lead to philosophical mistakes. In this way, Marx seems to anticipate some trends of Wittgenstein's reflection, particularly the idea that the main philosophical aim must be the critique of language (2001, §4.0031).

In doing this, I will try to bring to light and analyse some instances drawn from the section of *The German Ideology*, which is dedicated to the discussion of Stirner's book, *The Unique and his property*. Given that this section has been traditionally underestimated in the Marxist debate as it is considered less relevant than the first, more well known section dedicated to Feuerbach (Merker, 2010, p. 68), I will try to restore its relevance. As already noted by Rossi-Landi (1966, p. 205), in this section it is quite evident how the critique of ideology can be understood not only as the critique of philosophical language, but as the critique of some uses of language that contribute to the formation of a philosophical system separated from reality. The main advantage of starting from this section is that here, the term "ideology" and the "ideological representations" do not entail a problematic philosophy of history as found in the more problematic section dedicated to Feuerbach, which will not be discussed here. For this reason, this section will be considered as an autonomous part of *The German Ideology*.

In the second part of this contribution, I would on the one hand like to stress the evident antipsychologism in Marx's thought and, on the other, use Wittgenstein's concept of the language game in reading Marx's works. In this way, I will try to not only bring up some Marxian suggestions on the relationship between language and action, but also show how Marx's analysis of our social forms of life allows the radicalization of Wittgenstein's conception of language games in a social key normally neglected by Wittgenstein and Wittgensteinians.

2. Marx and Wittgenstein on language and philosophy

2.1. The mystification of language

In the *Preface* of his *Tractatus logico-philosophicus*, Wittgenstein introduces his book in the following way: "[it] deals with the problems of philosophy, and shows, I believe, that the reason why these problems are posed is that the logic of our language is misunderstood" (2001, p. 3). With these few words, the radical philosophical revolution called "linguistic turn" finds its beginning. It is characterized not only by the shifting of focus from the "being" and the "thought" towards the "language", but also by a radical reconfiguration of the status and the primary function of the philosophical work. Wittgenstein states in the proposition 4.002: "Language disguises thought. So much so, that from the outward form of the clothing it is impossible to infer the form of the thought beneath it, because the outward form of the clothing is not designed to reveal the form of the body, but for entirely different purposes" (*ibid.*, §4.002). In the following propositions (*ibid.*, §4.003; 4.0031) Wittgenstein refers to most of the philosophical propositions as "nonsensical" and presents the new task of philosophy as "critique of language". In other words, the new task of philosophers is not to philosophise more, but to clarify and criticize what has already been done with philosophy.

Despite the radical difference of conceiving language between the first and the second Wittgenstein, there is a clear continuity between the two phases of Wittgenstein's thought in the way to conceive the role of philosophy. As in *Tractatus*, and even in *Philosophical Investigations,* the focus is thus on showing how philosophical non-sense, errors, and philosophical problems arise from a misunderstanding of our language. Philosophy does not aim to explain, but only to describe the world (Wittgenstein, 1958, §109, 126) and in this way it is "a battle against the bewitchment of our intelligence by means of language" (*ibid.*, §109). If we were to ask why language tends to deceive us, Wittgenstein would call into play "einen Trieb, es misszuverstehen" [an urge to misunderstand it] (*ibid.*). Language appears to be the disease and the therapy at the same time, for this reason, if "philosophers use a word –'knowledge', 'being', 'Object', 'I', 'proposition', 'name' and try to grasp the essence of the thing", the new goal of philosophy should be "to bring words back from their metaphysical to their everyday use" (*ibid.*, §116). In this everyday use, the key to solving these philosophical misunderstandings could be found.

Starting from this assumption, let us now turn to the following question: what does Marx share with this new conception of philosophy? Despite the clear difference between the two philosophers, according to Boudon (1991), Marx can be considered as part of a philosophical tradition, according to which, to clarify our thought means to clarify the language that expresses these thoughts. As does Wittgenstein, in his critique of ideologies, Marx attempts to reveal the deceptions, the errors and the illusions that bring humans to have some ideological representations of the world. In this way, Wittgenstein's conception, according to which, philosophical investigations must "shed light on our problem by clearing misunderstandings away" (*ibid.*, §90) may be compared to Marx's critique of ideology. With "ideology", in fact, Marx refers to the set of our representations where "men and their relations appear upside-down as in a *camera obscura*" (Marx and Engels, 2010b, p. 36) so that individuals refer to reality in an inverted way.[1] Using Wittgenstein's words, ideological representations can be described as pictures that "held us captive" (*ibid.*, §115), but also as a "pair of glasses on our nose through which we see whatever we look at" (Wittgenstein, 1958, §103).

Like Wittgenstein, Marx tries to explain the reason why "it never occurs to us to take them off" (*ibid.*, §103), but his answer may not be reduced to the individuation of a "Trieb" (instinct). According to Marx, and in contrast to Wittgenstein, in order to clarify these "pictures" or "representations", the analysis has to start from the material, social and historical circumstances in which these "pictures" are generated. This attempt is made in his materialistic conception about the genesis of ideas. However, since Marx compares this inversion to that "of objects on the retina" (*ibid.*) and that the retina is the physiological "medium" through which an external fact is grasped by human mind, I would like to show how in Marx's view, language, as a natural and historical device, contributes in a relevant way to producing this ideological inversion. In this way, material conditions and a particular way to use language develop some philosophical errors that contribute to distorting how individuals relate to each other. Marx stresses how a critique of the use of words is potentially in strict relation with a critique of the social circumstances in which these words are used.

2.2. *The critique of the previous philosophy*

The critique of ideologies is the critique of previous philosophical systems, a critique that will be extended to the economic theories in his later writings. As in Wittgensteins', in Marx's critique of the previous philosophy a key role is played by the critique of the linguistic forms used by ideologists, as well as the logical errors made by them. Philosophy seems to be conceived, at least in these early writings, not as a doctrine as much as a critical activity, whose main purpose is "a clarification of our thoughts". What has to be clarified is not only how these thoughts are generated by materialistic conditions and how they contribute to concealing the real social relationship, but also, I will add, what role is played by language.

---

1   This inversion can be regarded in two different ways, firstly, as the process where consciousness is grasped as separated from social practices, so that the thought's realm seems to be autonomous from the historical process of human social life (cfr. Eagleton, 1991, pp. 70-71); secondly, inversion is the process in which the consequence (what historically comes after) is confused with the cause (what historically comes before) (cfr. Merker, 2010, p. 69).

In Marx's early works, the *pars destruens* is prominent to the *costruens*. In writings such as *Critique of Hegel's Philosophy of Right* (1843), *On the Jewish Question* (1843), *The Holy Family* (1845), *The Poverty of Philosophy* (1847), Marx builds his own position by criticizing the philosophy of his time. This aspect will never be lost; rather, it will be extended to areas other than the philosophical one. Since in his work Marx underlines how the "idea's realm" is generated by real contradictions, he stresses the relevance of detecting philosophical errors "mental cramps" as symptoms of real contradictions, in order to start a practical change of this reality. If Wittgenstein says that philosophical mistakes are due to the fact that "language goes on holiday" (1958, §38), Marx more likely focuses on the practical reasons and conditions that contribute to this holiday of language.

Marx's fight against ideologies is the fight against such theories that supposedly describe reality, yet seem to be disconnected from it and therefore mystify it. For Marx, the subject of this mystification is not the dominant class *per se* - which intentionally misleads reality- as much as it is the whole social system, whose capitalists are only, as Marx will say in *Capital*, social masks of the social relation of production.

In all of his philosophical production, Marx stresses how linguistic ambiguities contribute to misleading the bourgeois theorists so that their theoretical confusion is functional to the *status quo*, as well as these linguistic ambiguities being used to offer a description of reality that does not correspond with it.

However, Marx does not seem to understand philosophy *per se* as an ideological form, but only a particular philosophy, the idealistic one. The problem here is what is it that makes a philosophy idealistic. Wittgenstein criticizes the investigation of the essence of the thing (its metaphysical use) (*ibid.*, §116), whereas Marx's critique of Idealism refers to the sublimation's process of the concepts (cfr. Marx and Engels, 2010b, p. 36).

The critique of philosophy is the critique of the omnipotence of ideas, when these are considered as "absolute", that is, as they *were* released from reality (*ibid.*, p. 357). For this reason, in Marx's writings idealism seems to lose the connotations of a specific philosophy, since all the previous philosophies seem to be affected from an idealistic point of view in the way they deal with their own concepts. As in Wittgenstein, this "trieb" leads to some concepts being shifted from their everyday use to a metaphysical level, introducing a distinction between the real world and the ideal one.

In these writings, the split from the previous philosophical tradition takes the form of a real hand-to-hand that Marx undertakes without exception with the various authors that he brought back to idealism. For us today, the ferocious and decidedly derisory way in which Marx debates with his opponents may seem surprising. This applies not only to *The German Ideology*, but also to works such as *The Jewish Question*, *Critique of Hegel's Philosophy of Right* and *The Holy Family*. In these works, Marx progressively seems to reach his philosophical position from the reconstruction of the proverbial rubble he left lying around.

2.3. *When "language goes on holiday": sophisms and logical errors of ideologies in Marx*

The fight against ideologues has to be understood as the attempt to ridicule the confused arguments, the "sophisms", and the "canonisation" of universal terms, which lead to "philosophical non-sense" (Marx and Engels, 2010b, pp.360, 362, 390). In an emblematic way, Marx will present this point of view in the title of a 1848 work, where Marx makes fun of Proudhon's work *The Philosophy of Poverty* by showing how rough argumentation based on an imprecise use of language leads to the "poverty of philosophy".

But it is in the section dedicated to Stirner that the most relevant contribution to this topic can be found: "In direct contrast to German philosophy which descends from heaven to earth, here it is a matter of ascending from earth to heaven. That is to say, not of setting out from what men say, imagine, conceive, nor from men as narrated, thought of, imagined, conceived, in order to arrive at men in the flesh..." (Marx and Engels, 2010b, p. 36). Marx starts from the critique of the propositional contents of our imagination and our thoughts in order to make evident how these contents do not ultimately grasp the reality they pretend to grasp. However, this is only the initial step in Marx's analysis, because the following step is to understand, firstly, what these contents actually express, and secondly, why they express their content in an inverted way.

In Marx, the critique of ideas is surely not enough, however, it is the first step in making the workers conscious of the real nature of the social relationship in which they are involved. In this way, the critique and analysis of ideas correspond to the description of the "genesis" of these ideas. This "genesis" calls into play the form of life in which a word is used and how, that is, their specific (historical and institutional) context of use.

In the section dedicated to the discussion of *The unique* of Stirner, Marx does not only stress how many philosophical errors and confusions are attributed to certain linguistic ambiguities, but also identifies different examples of "logical" or "speculative trick" (*ibid.*, pp. 62, 99,100,103, 110, 114 274), "logical swindle" (*ibid.*, p. 287) that contribute to the development of a thought (philosophy) that Marx defines as "beggar's broth" (*ibid.*, pp. 235, 272, 427).

2.4. *The method of appositions and other logical tricks*

In Marx's argumentation, a very special role is played by what he calls "method of appositions" (*ibid.*, p. 156) presented as the "logical and historical locomotive, the driving force of the [Stirner's] book" (*ibid.*, p. 274), that is described in the following way:

> In order to transform one idea into another, or to prove the identity of two quite different things, a few intermediate links are sought which partly by their meaning, partly by their etymology and partly by their mere sound can be used to establish an apparent connection between the two basic ideas. These links are then appended to the first idea in the form of an apposition, and in such a way that one gets farther and farther away from the starting-point and nearer and nearer to the point one wants to reach. (*ibid.*, pp. 274-75)

In this kind of argumentative process the conceptual development occurs by "jumps", as the passages are not justified and the two ideas are combined by virtue of the similarities of their signifiers. Indeed, "alongside the apposition", where several ideas, even if opposite each other, are brought back to a single sense, Marx continues, "we have the *synonymy*" that specifies the first in a particular way: "If two words are etymologically linked or are merely similar in sound, they are made responsible for each other…" (*ibid.*, p. 274). The "etymological synonymy" consists in the connections of two ideas based on the simple assonances of some sounds (*ibid.*, p. 276). In the case of Stirner, it is clearly understood how the use of "logical tricks" (erroneous etymology, ambiguous meanings) contribute, in Marx's view, to the constitution of ideology. In a passage of his book, Stirner argues against those authors, who emphasise the relevance of society in contrast to the individual, the egoist. He states, in fact, «every people, every state is injurious to the individual» (Stirner, 2017, p. 228). Stirner warns of the danger of the primate of collective subject, the Nation, the State, the *Volk*, because the good for the Volk does not correspond to the good of the individual. A liberty of the people, he continues, is not a liberty of the individual. The example Marx uses is that of *Gesellschaft*, which, according to Stirner, derived from *Sal* (building), and is wrongly conceived as being derived from *Saal* (salon). Marx states that this combination of the two words proposed by Stirner is used to criticize the term *Gesellschaft* used by communists. Stirner says that "those who are in the room are in society even as mute persons" and "when it comes to actual intercourse, this is to be regarded as independent of society;" (*ibid.*, p. 229). In this way, Stirner's attempt is to reduce the concept of "society" to the "civil society" of Hegel, as an assemblage of individuals who are independent from each other. The wrong etymology presented is, thus, functional to his aim: the critique of communist concept of society.

> Synonymy serves our saint, on the one hand, to transform empirical relations into speculative relations, by using in its speculative meaning a word that occurs both in practical life and in philosophical speculation, uttering a few phrases about this speculative meaning and then making out that he has thereby also criticised the actual relations which this word denotes as well. (Marx and Engels, 2010b, p. 277)

In doing so, according to Marx, Stirner, instead of criticizing the economic system, transforms "bourgeois relations (…) into personal, individual relations, which one cannot attack without attacking the individuality, 'peculiarity' and 'uniqueness' of the individual" (Ibid.). What is historically grounded is, thus, naturalized and is made possible by an erroneous reconstruction of the genesis of these words and concepts.

This is quite evident in another very interesting passage where Marx refers to Destutt de Tracy:

> For the bourgeois it is all the easier to prove on the basis of his language the identity of commercial and individual, or even universal, human relations, as this language itself is a product of the bourgeoisie, and therefore both in actuality and in language the relations of buying and selling have been made the basis of all others. For example, *propriété*—property *[Eigentum]* and characteristic feature *[Eigenschaft]*; property—possession *[Eigentum]* and peculiarity *[Eigentümlichkeit]*; *"eigen"* ["one's own"]—in the commercial and in the individual sense; *valeur,* value, *Wertb;* commerce, *Verkehrc; échange, exchange, Austausch6,* etc., all of which are used both for commercial relations and for characteristic features and mutual relations of individuals as such. (…) Our kindly, credulous Jacques takes the bourgeois play on the words Eigentum [property] and Eigenschaft [characteristic feature] so literally, in such holy earnest, that he even endeavours to behave like a private property-owner in relation to his own features, as we shall see later on. (*Ibid.*, p. 231)

Marx shows how the values of the bourgeois ideologists are reflected in language (*ibid.*, p. 277). The signifier *Eigentum* (private property), in fact, is traced back to a semantic constellation, in which both *eigen* (proper), understood as what is proper, and *Eigenschaften* (quality), understood as qualities proper to the subject, are included.

> This [trick consists] in seizing on [*one* aspect], treating it as if it were the sole [and only] aspect so far known of an idea [or] concept which [has several well]-defined aspects, foisting this aspect [on the concept as] its *sole characteristic* and then setting [against it every other] aspect under a [new name, as] something original. (*Ibid.*, p. 273)

In this way, the historical and social institution of "private property", precisely by virtue of its signifier, is conceived as a fundamental characteristic of the individual *per se*, that is, the "proper". In Stirners argumentation, the paradox arises that, in order for the individual to humanly establish himself, he must first establish himself as bourgeois. This is allowed by the appositions used in order to justify the social institution of private property with the abstract notion of "proper" (*ibid.*, p. 229). A second example is the term "exchange". In Smith's *The Wealth of Nations*, the exchange between private owners is naturalised through an analogy of linguistic exchange, indeed the "exchange" between private owners is derived, and in this way legitimized, directly from a natural predisposition to the linguistic "exchanges". The juxtaposition between a species-specific human property and a historically determined activity is functional to the naturalisation of bourgeois production relations based on the economic exchanges. Marx notes that this sort of lexical (and ideological) ambiguity can be found in French, English and German, since the terms *Austausch, exchange, échange* terms "are used both for commercial relations and for characteristic features and mutual relations of individuals as such" (*ibid.*, p. 231).

In this way, the use of the same signifier (*Austausch*) leads to a dulling of the different signifieds and so, this semantic reductionism is functional to the application of the method of apposition (man has a natural predisposition to the exchanges, economic exchanges are a human property, what is properly human is the private property), from which ideology arises. In this way, different forms of life (in this case: forms of exchange) are traced back to a single one (the forms of exchange typical of the capitalist society), the semantic hierarchy becomes the mirror image of the social and political hierarchy, and the former contributes to concealing the latter.

As noted by different scholars, Marx presupposes thus a theory of meaning, according to which, meaning is determined by external *material* conditions (Rubinstein, 1981; Wilkie, 1976, p. 236f.). As underlined by Vološinov, the material dimension of the signifier turns the sign (and the corresponding signified) into the object of the historical transformation (Vološinov, 1982, p. 10). The sign is not the manifestation of a psychological entity, but is the historical and social product of human interactions, by their *Verkehr*. Let us consider this passage where Marx objects to Stirner that:

> He identifies first of all "owning" as a private property-owner with "owning" in general. Instead of examining the definite relations between private property and production, instead of examining "owning" as a landed proprietor, as a rentier, as a merchant, as a factory-owner, as a worker—where "owning" would be found to be a quite distinct kind of owning, control over other people's labour—he transforms all these relations into "owning as such". (Marx and Engels, 2010b, p. 206)

In contrast to Stirner, Marx underlines how the meaning of the verb "to own" depends on who the subject is that "owns". In other words, grammatically, the verb "to own" is neutral, but once it is used in a specific context, its meaning is subjected to some oscillations of sense. Behind the same verb different kinds of possession are concealed and are thus deleted and neutralized as if they were all the same.[2] This dulling of the differences leads to an ideological representation because the use of the verb "own" is no longer able to grasp the specificity of the situation to which it refers. In this particular use of the word, I do not simply describe reality, but I reduce different forms of possession to an ideal one.

---

2   Obviously, Marx's analysis of language concentrates on a particular vocabulary and is not as general as in Wittgenstein's work. Marx's attention to a verb like "to have" in contrast to the verb "to be" reflects one of the major differences between Marx and Wittgenstein, the former being more focused on political, social and economic topics (cfr. Cook, 1982), the latter on logical and ethical problems. For example, Wittgenstein states that «in common language it is very frequent that the same word designates differently (...) or that two words (...) are applied in the same way in the proposition» (1958, § 3.323). In this example Wittgenstein refers to the verb "to be" which can be used as a sign of equality, copulation, or expression of existence. With this example, Wittgenstein underlines how a semantic ambiguity can be the basis of a real philosophical misunderstanding.

3. *The radical anti-psychologism in Marx's analysis of capitalism*

3.1. *From the analysis of meaning to the analysis of human forms of social life*

Since the analysis of the meaning of signs requires placing emphasis on the social conditions in which signs are used, in Marx the critique of the use of language is combined with the critique of human forms of social life. In this second part, I will draw attention to how this approach can be found even in Marx's mature critique of political economy and that his analysis of the capitalist mode of production leads to the broadening of the boundaries of Wittgenstein's concept of "language game", revealing his potential for the analysis of society.

In *Philosophical Investigations,* Wittgenstein presents a list of instances, in order to understand what he intends with "language-games". They are simple actions such as "the process of naming the stones and of repeating words after someone" (1958, §7), more complicated actions such as "forming and testing a hypothesis" or "solving a problem in practical arithmetic" (*ibid.,* §23), and wider cases such as "building a bridge or a machine"(*ibid.,* §364). But examples of language-games are also speech acts like "asking, thanking, cursing, greeting, praying" (*ibid.,* §23). This concept has no precise boundaries (*ibid.,* §17,19,23) as it is necessary to emphasise not only the different ways in which language is used, but also that language can not be conceived separately from the praxis, since it is interwoven with action. Wittgenstein's conception of language games strongly influenced subsequent philosophers of language such as Austin and Searle. However, in their theories of speech acts they tried to circumscribe it. With both philosophers, the main purpose is to offer a classification of the different kinds of illocutionary acts that could be produced (Searle, 1979, p. 1). This attempt has always led to drawing the attention towards what the speaker *wants* to express and how the hearer *interprets* the content of the speaker. Within this framework, the focus is not so much on the linguistic *situation* in which the speaker operates, but on what the *speaker* does when talking. This is quite evident in Searle's taxonomy of speech acts where the first three criteria chosen are centralised on the purpose and the psychological state (*ibid.*, pp 2ff.) of the individual that is talking. In Searle, the "Theory of speech acts" is characterized by an intentionalistic turn estranged from Wittgenstein's conception, and in which history and social practice are relegated to the background.

On the contrary, even if Wittgenstein does not seem to be so interested in taking into account language games which are characterized by historically determined coordinates, his notion of the language game is intertwined with the whole linguistic situation in which individuals operate, so that, "to imagine a language means to imagine a form of life" (1958, §19). In this way, the focus is not only on *what* the individuals do, but also on the *context* they operate in and under which circumstances. However, the "forms of life" analysed by Wittgenstein are always circumscribed situations and, therefore, are not considered as political or historical aspects. In contrast to an intentionalistic turn, an anthropological turn can be found in Wittgenstein's *Philosophical Investigations*, where the new role of philosophy is that of putting "everything before us, and neither explains nor deduces anything" (*ibid.*, §126).

Moreover, as many scholars have noted, Wittgenstein and Marx seem to diverge radically on this point. In contrast to what Wittgenstein supposes, in Marx the description seems to always be finalized by the transformation of the reality.[3] However, I would highlight how the transformation of reality in Marx has to be realized practically and not philosophically. Accordingly, philosophy (or at least philosophy as critical activity) has to describe reality in order to make the individual aware of the real contradictions of the situation they are involved in, because *only after* would they be able to change it. From this point of view, an anthropological turn in the young Marx can also be found. In the section dedicated to Stirner, Marx states in a paradigmatic way the relevance of "the study of the actual world" (Marx and Engels, 2010b, p. 236), that has the same relation to speculative philosophy "as onanism and sexual love" (*ibid.*). He still affirms "one has to 'leave philosophy aside' (…), one has to leap out of it and devote oneself like an ordinary man to the study of actuality, for which there exists also an enormous amount of literary material, unknown, of course, to the philosophers" (*ibid.*). For this reason, Marx's direction is not so much an abandonment of philosophy as such, but a rethinking of the function of philosophy as a critique of all those discourses that conceal reality and abstract from it. To this "literary" material, we could add historical, anthropological and economic material; because only by studying this material is it possible to answer the question: "how did it come about that people 'got' these illusions 'into their heads'"? (*ibid.*). If we try to follow

---

3   This is true at least for the young Marx, while in the mature Marx the discovery of the contradictory character of (social) reality will require an "explanation" of what appears.

this question, we can find continuity in Marx's thought even if the kind of the answer offered changes in a radical way over the course of time.[4]

I will now try to begin from a particular case taken from the *Comments on James Mill, Élémens d'économie politique*. Here Marx considers a situation that can be described as a language game (in particular a speech act). The case is the following:

> The only intelligible language in which we converse with one another consists of our objects in their relation to each other. We would not understand a human language and it would remain without effect. By one side it would be recognised and felt as being a request, an entreaty, and therefore a *humiliation,* and consequently uttered with a feeling of shame, of degradation. By the other side it would be regarded as *impudence* or *lunacy* and rejected as such. We are to such an extent estranged from man's essential nature that the direct language of this essential nature seems to us a *violation of human dignity,* whereas the estranged language of material values seems to be the well-justified assertion of human dignity that is self-confident and conscious of itself. (Marx, 2010a, p. 227)

This situation can be described as a language game with two actors, where *A* says something to *B*, in order to influence his behaviour and *B* reacts to *A*'s request. This language-game (α) coincides with a speech act such as a "request". Since this request is not explicitly expressed, it could be so formulated "A needs X and asks B for it, as B has X".

---

4   In this way, there is continuity in Marx's thought in his attempt to criticize the linguistic forms through which we try to describe reality. However, if in the young Marx the main problem is represented by political and philosophical ideology, in the mature Marx the main target is the ideological theories of certain political economists. Obviously, there are some very important differences because, as Althusser points out: "The Young Marx of the 1844 Manuscripts read the human essence at sight, immediately, in the transparency of its alienation. Capital, on the contrary, exactly measures a distance and an internal dislocation in the real, inscribed in its structure, a distance and a dislocation such as to make their own effects themselves illegible, and the illusion of an immediate reading of them the ultimate apex of their effects: fetishism" (Althusser, 1970, p. 18). So, if in his early writings we find the redundant reference to the "facts", in *Capital* the problem is represented from these "facts" themselves: "Man's reflections on the forms of social life, and consequently, also, his scientific analysis of those forms, take a course directly opposite to that of their actual historical development. He begins, post festum with the results of the process of development ready at hand before him.(…) It is, however, just this ultimate money form of the world of commodities that actually conceals, instead of disclosing, the social character of private labour, and the social relations between the individual producers" (Marx, 2010b, p. 86).

Marx's analysis tries to emphasise how the different ways this content is understood by both parts is dependent on the social circumstances: B conceives this speech act as an inappropriate request from A, which he *should* not do, and for this reason this request is grasped as a form of impudence and, conversely, A feels ashamed. In the situation described by Marx, this speech act is a directive, and in particular a plea. If we ask ourselves how a simple request or an order differentiates from a plea, we could answer that even if a request such as the plea refers to asking for something that A doesn't have and is owned by B, there is a clear difference between these two kinds of speech acts: in the former, A may have good reasons to believe that his request can be satisfied (order), or at least, there is a pair relation between the interlocutors (simple request). On the contrary, the latter is characterised by the subordination of one part to the other. In order to grasp this language game, it has to be contextualized into a wider form of life that coincides with what Marx calls capitalistic mode of production.

Let's now imagine a radically different situation (β) in which B interprets A's request, not as a form of humiliation/impudence, but as something that is his duty to satisfy because it expresses the human essence consisting in mutual supports. In order to understand the difference between the situations α and β, the language used, the different kind of relationship between the two actors and the different way the actors engage each other, we should imagine two radically different forms of life. Marx's analysis of the mode of production as a form of life allows the answering of the question: "how did it come about that people 'got' these illusions 'into their heads'". The analysis of what individuals think or say requires reference to the wider context of use.

3.2. *Theory of value and language*

In order to understand the capitalistic mode of production and how it determines human forms of thought, a key role is played by Marx's conception of value developed in his mature writings. In our daily language we are used to *saying* that money and commodities "have" a value and for this reason we are led to believe that "exchange value" is an intrinsic characteristic of things, and that commodities appear to be contradictory things because they are exchange value and use value at the same time.

On the one hand, it is our daily language that contributes to deceiving us, on the other hand, according to Marx, this linguistic confusion and contradiction is grounded on a real contradiction. Since in the capitalist system the socialization of our private labour is realized *ex post* though the relations of our things, the latter assume social properties.

The "value form" is in fact, according to Marx, the "form" though which "entering into *direct* production relations with his buyers B, C and D, our commodity producer A is actually connected, by a thick network of *indirect* production relations, with innumerable other people (…), in the final analysis, with all members of society" (Rubin, 1990, p. 8).

In this way, this socialization occurs behind the backs of the social actors (Marx, 2010b, p. 97). Marx's theory of value presupposes a radical discrepancy between what a human being does individually, what he individually thinks of his action and what individuals do as parts of a social system: "the separate commodity producer, formally independent from others in terms of the orientation, extent and methods of his production, is actually closely related to them through the market, through exchange" (Rubin, 1990, p. 9).

In the realization of the social synthesis behind the back of the individual, a key role is played by language. First of all, in order to establish the world of commodities, "the commodities are first transformed into bars in the head and in speech before they are exchanged for one another. They are appraised before being exchanged, and in order to appraise them they must be brought into a given numerical relation to one another. In order to bring them into such a numerical relation, in order to make them commensurable, they must obtain the same denomination (unit)" (Marx, 1973, p. 80). Secondly, the exchange value, in the form of the price, allows the comparison of commodities to each other, so that the system of price operates as a semantic system. Thirdly, language allows the passage from the "universal equivalent form" to the money in which "the character of direct and universal exchangeability — in other words, that the universal equivalent form — has now, by social custom, become finally identified with the substance, gold" (Marx, 2010b, pp. 80-81). Each of these situations can be described as being different kinds of language games, where language and action are interwoven. However, nobody can be considered alone, but only in relation to others. In these cases, the attention is not only on what the social actors do with language, but also how language operates behind the back of the individual.

For this reason, as stressed by scholars like Rubin (1990), Backhaus (1997) and Reichelt (2001), Marx's analysis of value in *Capital* cannot be reduced to an economic presentation of a "traditional" quantitative theory of value, as many economists such as Böhm-Bawerk (1896) did. In the first pages of the first book of *Capital*, Marx develops a sociological analysis of how human relations take the form of relations amongst things and for this reason, as Rubin suggested, the paragraph on the fetishism of commodities is to be understood as the cornerstone of Marx's analysis of value (Rubin, 1990, p. 5). In this way, we deal with a social ontology, even if "inverted"[5], since the "objects" can be grasped as "social" only because individuals don't know exactly what they're doing in the commodities exchange. From this inverted situation, the economic categories even if seem to refer directly to entities of the world –according to a correspondence theory of the meaning – contribute to concealing reality rather than to describing it, and in this way the real contradictions are translated into logical and linguistic contradictions[6].

For this reason, Marx tries to criticize those economic theories that take this contradictory (social) reality as the point of departure for their analysis, rather than try to explain it. But this explanation does not correspond to the abandonment of reality, demanding a return to the ivory tower of speculation. On the contrary, it corresponds to the need to understand how our social action, that which cannot be reduced to the simple sum of the singulars, shapes our reality and our representations of it.

The real actor in Marx's analysis is not the individual but the whole social system, realized by the radical social nature of language, that is, the system of prices. It is for this reason that what they individually do or say is not at stake, but it is what happens behind their backs that determines their intentions and their representations of what they do.

For this reason, in the first pages of *Capital*, individuals are not mentioned, because, as Marx will state later, they are reduced to social masks. If some scholars and economists have found in this the main problem and limit of Marx's economic analysis, on the contrary, it allows us to highlight the radical social antipsychologism at the base of Marx's analysis.

4. *Conclusion*

In this contribution, I have tried to underline two aspects of Marx's thought that I believe are relevant for philosophy of language. The first one is that in Stirner's section of *The German Ideology*, Marx focused on the critique of some "liberal" uses of language that lead to what he calls

---

5   This in contrast to the contemporary debate on social ontology developed into analytical debate (cfr. Searle 1995, 2010).

6   Use value/exchange value; concrete labour/ abstract labour.

"ideology". In this way, the concept of ideology is not conceived into the framework of a philosophy of history, according to which, ideology arose in a particular historical moment and could have been overcome in the future, since the critique of ideology seems to correspond to a critique of philosophical language, characterized by the attempt to escape from reality. In other words, when Marx stresses the relevance of the materialistic genesis of our ideas, he sheds light on the use of context and social circumstances in which our ideas, concepts, representations and at least meanings are shaped.

Beginning with these assumptions, Marx seems to anticipate the key suggestion of Wittgenstein, according to which the critique of our thought is possible through the critique of our language. However, given that Marx's critique of language is combined with the critique and analysis of the social circumstances, and the material conditions in which our "ideas" are formed, he could help to reveal the social potential of a critique of language.

Secondly, what I believe that Marx and Wittgenstein have in common is their approach - even if elaborated differently - to the way of conceiving the relation between language and action. Obviously, Marx is not a philosopher of language in the terms of the Austrian philosopher, however, in Marx's analysis of the capitalistic system of production, where the attention is focused on how human social relations are realized through things, language plays a key role. It is called into play not only in Marx's critique of vulgar economists, grounded by the idea that the descriptions and the categories used conceal reality, but also in a very different way in order to organize the social synthesis behind the backs of social actors. The antipsychologism of Marx sets language free from the restricted boundaries of the individual mind, making it the logical and public space into which the relationships among individuals are constituted.

References

Althusser L. (1968). *Reading Capital*. Paris: François Maspero.

Backhaus H.G. (1997) *Dialektik der Wertform: Untersuchungen zur Marxschen Ökonomiekritik*. Freiburg: ça ira Verlag.

Böhm-Bawerk, E. von (1896) *Zum Abschluss des Marxschen System*. Freiburg: O. Haering.

Boudon R. (1991). *L'ideologia. Origine dei pregiudizi*. Torino: Einaudi.

Cook D. (1982). Marx's Critique of Philosophical Language. *Philosophy and Phenomenological Research*, 42, pp. 530-554.

De Iaco M. (2019). Wittgenstein to Sraffa: two newly-discovered letters from February and March 1934. In *Nordic Wittgenstein Review*, vol. 8, no. 1-2, pp. 209-223, 2019.

Eagleton T. (1991) *Ideology. An introduction*. London/New York: Verso.

Fineschi R. (2017). Produzione materiale e produzione linguistica tra Marx e Rossi-Landi. Rileggendo "Il linguaggio come lavoro e come mercato". In G. Borrelli, A. Santangelo, G. Sgrò (Eds.) *Il valore nel linguaggio e nell'economia*. Tricase (Le): Libellula, pp. 105-120.

Gakis D. (2015). Wittgenstein, Marx and Marxism: Some Historical Connections. In *Humanities*, Vol. 4, No. 4, pp. 924-937.

Garofalo P. (in press). Language, thought and reality in Marx's German Ideology and in the mature critique of political economy. In F. Sulpizio, M. De Iaco, G. Schimmenti (Eds.) *Wittgenstin and Marx. Marx and Wittgenstein*. Peter Lang.

Kitching G., Pleasants N. (Eds.) (2002). *Marx and Wittgenstein. Knowledge, morality and politics*. New York: Routledge.

Lo Piparo F. (2010). Gramsci and Wittgenstein: an Intriguing Connection. In A. Capone (Ed.), *Perspectives on Language Use and Pragmatics. A volume in Memory of Sorin Stati*. Munich: Lincom Europa Academic Publications, pp. 285-319.

Marjanović A. (2005). Introduzione alla vita e alle carte di Raffaello Piccoli: un racconto. In *Cartevive. Periodico dell'Archivio Prezzolini*, I, Giugno, 2005, pp. 26-84.

Marx K. (1973). *Grundrisse: foundations of the critique of political economy*. London: Peguin Book

Marx K. (2010a). Comments on James Mill., Élémens d'économie politique. In K. Marx & F. Engels, *Collected Works* (Vol. 3). London: Lawrence & Wishart.

Marx, K. (2010b). Capital. Volume I. In K. Marx & F. Engels, *Collected Works* (Vol. 35). London: Lawrence & Wishart.

Marx, K. and Engels, F. (2010a). The German Ideology. In K. Marx & F. Engels, *Collected Works* (Vol. 5). London: Lawrence & Wishart.

Marx K. and Engels (2010b). The holy family. In K. Marx & F. Engels, *Collected Works* (Vol. 4). London: Lawrence & Wishart.

Merker N. (2011) *Karl Marx. Vita e opera*. Roma-Bari: Laterza.

Newmeyer F. J. (1977) Reviewed Work: Linguistics and Economics by Ferruccio Rossi-Landi, Language, Vol. 53, No. 1 (Mar., 1977), pp. 254-256. Published By: *Linguistic Society of America*: https://doi.org/10.2307/413078

Reichelt H. (2001) *Zur logischen Struktur des Kapitalbegriffs bei Karl Marx*. Freiburg: ça ira Verlag

Rossi-Landi F. (1966). Toward a Marxian Use of Wittgenstein. In G. Kitching and N. Pleasants (Eds), *Marx and Wittgenstein; Knowledge, Morality and Politics*. London: Routledge, 2002, pp.185-212.

Rubin I.I. (1990). *Essays on Marx's theory of value*. Montréal-New York: Black Rose Book.

Rubinstein D. (1981). *Marx and Wittgenstein. Social Praxis and Social Explanation*. London-Boston: Routledge & Kegan Paul.

Searle J. R. (1971). A taxonomy of illocutionary acts. In J. Searle, *Expression and meaning*. Cambridge University Press, 1979.

Sen A. (2003). Sraffa, Wittgenstein and Gramsci. In *Journal of Economic Literature*, vol. 41, pp. 1240-1255.

Sériot P. (2011). Vološinov, la philosophie du langage et le marxisme. In *Langages*, 2, pp. 83-96.

Stirner M. (2017). *The Unique and its property*. Baltimore: Underworld.

Vološinov V. (1982). *Marxism and the Philosophy of Language*. Cambridge: Harvard University Press.

Wittgenstein L. (1958). *Philosophical Investigations*, Basil Blackwell, Oxford.

Wittgenstein L. (2001). *Tractatus logico-philosophicus*. London and NewYork: Routldege.

3.
SUBJECTIVITY AND HUMAN AGENCY

DIMITRIS GAKIS

SUBJECTIVITY AND LATE CAPITALISM
From Marx to Wittgenstein

1. *Introduction: Marx(ism), Wittgenstein, and the question of human subjectivity*

Discussions pertaining to the issue of individual and collective subjectivity have been central to both Marxian and (post-)Marxist thought. Marx discusses issues connected to subjectivity, either explicitly or implicitly, throughout his oeuvre, while the whole diverse (post-) Marxist tradition – from Lukacs, the Frankfurt School of critical theory (Adorno, Horkheimer, Marcuse, Fromm), and the Praxis school (Petrovic) to the Situationist International (Debord), structuralism (Althusser), post-structuralism (Foucault, Deleuze, Derrida, Lyotard, Castoriadis), and Italian biopolitical theory (Agamben, Virno, Negri) – may be viewed as constitutively shaped by discussions of human subjectivity. While the thematics of subjectivity concerns a wide assortment of overlapping topics, such as human nature, (self-) consciousness, behavior, action and conduct, agency and intentionality, will and desire, identity and the self, phenomenal experience, and the relation between the mind, the body, and the world, or the 'inner' and the 'outer' – indicating the family resemblance character of the term 'subjectivity' –[1] one could say that in the end it designates a broad problematics revolving around the central question of philosophical anthropology, namely, what is, or what does it mean to be, a human being. From such a perspective, the question of human subjectivity synecdochically emerges also as one of the main motifs of Wittgenstein's later philosophy, paradigmatically demonstrated in the *Philosophical Investigations*, through his discussions of meaning and language, philosophy, logic and

---

1 Thus, 'subjectivity' is approached in this essay as a concept that does not identify a feature (or a single set of features) common to all different themes categorized under it, but "a complicated network of similarities overlapping and criss-crossing: sometimes overall similarities, sometimes similarities of detail" (Wittgenstein, 2001, §66).

mathematics, rule-following, psychological concepts (such as thinking, understanding, imagining, expecting, hoping, believing, willing, meaning, (self-)consciousness, intentionality), knowledge, certainty, etc. from an anthropological point of view.[2]

The goal of this short essay is to explore some of the affinities between the approaches of (the later) Wittgenstein and Marx to individual and collective human subjectivity and to also sketch some of the ways in which Wittgenstein's approach has influenced and may further compliment the (post-)Marxist, biopolitical analysis and critique of late capitalism. First, I discuss in the next section the congruent perspectives of Marx and (the later) Wittgenstein on language and consciousness as based on the everyday, the social and the practical, and the material. Then, I highlight in the third section how these perspectives reflect on their respective views on (the production of) individual and collective human subjectivity, especially in relation to human autonomy and corporeality, as manifestations of a radical critique of the Cartesian picture of subjectivity characterizing modernity. In the fourth and concluding section of the essay, I sketch how the analysis and critique of late capitalism, as shaped by biopolitical production, has been, and may be further, informed by the areas of overlap and complementarity between the approaches of (the later) Wittgenstein and Marx to (the production of) subjectivity, especially in regard to the emergence of the common as a social relation antagonistic to those of capital, property, and value.

2. *Marx and Wittgenstein on language and consciousness*

The starting point of our discussion of the points of convergence between Marx and the later Wittgenstein in regard to language and consciousness is to be found in their shared views on the mystifying character of (metaphysical) philosophical language and their consequent emphasis on

---

2   While Wittgenstein engages with the issue of subjectivity in his early writings
     (i.e., *Tractatus Logico-Philosophicus* and his early notebooks) too – in a rather
     Schopenhauerian manner – the anthropological perspective is a distinctive
     characteristic of his later thought. In the preface to the *Investigations*, Wittgenstein
     refers to his discussions with the renowned Italian Marxist economist (and friend
     of Gramsci) Piero Sraffa as the main stimulus for the most significant ideas
     presented in the work (see Wittgenstein, 2001, p. x), with the most important thing
     gaining from those discussions being an anthropological way of looking at
     philosophical problems (see Monk, 1991, p. 261).

and prioritization of everyday language, as well as in the metaphilosophical implications of these views. Marx holds that philosophical language and consciousness, in their manifestation as metaphysics and similarly to the language and consciousness of (bourgeois) politics, economics, law, etc., are reified/alienated forms of everyday language – the "language of reality" or the "language of real life" – and consciousness, which are expressions of human material/practical activity (see Marx and Engels, 1998, pp. 36, 42, 44, 248, 385, 475). They are alienated forms, because in philosophy (as metaphysics) words and consciousness are separated from life, taking an independent existence, and this is why Marx calls philosophers to dissolve their language into everyday language in order to recognize it as the distorted language of actual life and world (see *ibid.*, pp. 472-73). At the same time, Marx is critical of the idea that consciousness and its products, in the form of concepts and words, are "the real chains of men" and that a fight against certain illusionary concepts and words, through the opposition of different concepts and words which, supposedly, in a magical, redeeming, mystical, and superlinguistic manner point from within thought and language to the actual world, may in fact lead to radical changes in our real existing life and world (see *ibid.*, pp. 35-36, 248, 473-75).[3] In a strikingly similar way, Wittgenstein too is critical of the philosophical uses of language (in the form of metaphysics) as products of abstraction, idealization, and reification, which give rise to certain illusions about language, the world, and ourselves, thus, in the end, mystifying them (see e.g. Wittgenstein, 2001, §94-§97, §101, §103-§107, §115, §436). To that kind of philosophy – also exemplified in his own earlier outlook as demonstrated in the *Tractatus* – where language, abstracted from its concrete, everyday, practical settings, is approached and used as an "engine idling", thus going "on holiday" and creating certain mystified forms of consciousness and metaphysical "houses of cards" (*ibid.*, §38, §88, §118, §132), the later Wittgenstein opposes his new approach as based on the description and clarification of how words are used in our everyday language (see *ibid.*, §108, §116, §120, §124, §134, §494). For Wittgenstein, like Marx, not just words have meaning only in the stream of life (see Wittgenstein, 1980b, §504, §687), but, also, there are no "super-concepts" which point from within philosophical (metaphysical) language in a quasi-transcendental manner to the structure and nature of language

---

3   In particular, Marx addresses his criticism against the Young Hegelians (Feuerbach, Bauer, Stirner) and the key role that concepts such as "man", "criticism", "ego" play in their respective critical philosophical systems.

and the world (see Wittgenstein, 2001, §97). That is one of the reasons why the later Wittgenstein famously calls, again like Marx, for bringing back words from their metaphysical to their everyday use (*ibid.*, §116).[4]

The second point of convergence between Marx and Wittgenstein may be traced to their shared views on the constitutively social and practical nature of language and consciousness. From his early writings to his later works, Marx emphasizes throughout his oeuvre that both language and consciousness are social products (see e.g. Marx, 1990, p. 167; 1992, p. 350; 1993, pp. 84, 490; 1994a; Marx and Engels, 1998, pp. 42, 49-50). In particular, Marx argues that human subjects are constitutively social, since they individuate themselves only in the midst of society and as members of human communities. Language and consciousness are produced and developed only from the necessity of intercourse between human beings and are individualized only on the background of a human community, of people living and talking together (see Marx and Engels, 1998, pp. 42, 49-50). Thus, the very idea of a private language or consciousness, of a language or consciousness as a product of an individual, is an absurdity (see Marx, 1993, pp. 84, 490). Furthermore, according to Marx, language is not (just) the (social) product of (socially produced) consciousness, but in fact language "*is* [emphasis in the original] practical, real consciousness that exists for other men as well, and only therefore does it also exist for me" (Marx and Engels, 1998, p. 49). Language and consciousness emerge thus as manifestations of social human activity, of praxis, and it is on this base that Marx makes the, rather radical, claim that "the *original* roots of all words are *verbs* [emphasis in the original]" (*ibid.*, p. 292). The resemblances between the above views of Marx and those of the later Wittgenstein on language and consciousness as constitutively social and practical are clear. Wittgenstein, through the concept and role of language games and form(s) of life, his approach to meaning as a matter of use and to rule-following and language (games) as practices, customs, institutions, and, foremost, through his famous criticism against the very idea of a private language, repeatedly emphasizes in the *Investigations* the inherently social nature of language and meaning as opposed to their reified conceptions (see e.g. Wittgenstein,

---

4   It should be noted that Marx's and Wittgenstein's shared critique of philosophical language and consciousness and prioritization of everyday language and practical activity is also illustrative of one of their main metaphilosophical similarities, namely, their common belief that the resolution, or rather, dissolution of philosophical problems is a matter of collective human praxis and, in particular, of a change in our forms of life and consciousness (see Marx, 1992, p. 354; 1994a; Marx and Engels, 1998, pp. 63-64; Wittgenstein, 1978, Part II §23; 1998, p. 70).

2001, §7, §19, §22-§23, §31, §41-§43, §49-§54, §68-§72, §80-§88, §99-§100, §120, §198-§199, §243-§315, §540). The same holds for the social nature of consciousness as we may see in Wittgenstein's discussions of pain behaviour, consciousness, phenomenal experience, and the self (see e.g. *ibid.*, §244-§249, §258-§269, §279-§280, §288-§292, §300-§302, §311, §398-§427), and in general in his rejection of the conception of a private inner realm in which consciousness and mental states occur and reside: "an inner process stands in need of outward criteria" (*ibid.*, §580). Furthermore, Wittgenstein's discussion of first-person verbal communication of pain as a sophisticated manifestation of pain, replacing instinctual nonverbal pain behavior (see *ibid.*, §244-§249) may be viewed as highlighting, in a similar manner to Marx, a conception of language as practical consciousness, as well as an approach to language and consciousness as manifestations of social human activity (see also *ibid.*, §412-§427). For Wittgenstein, words are deeds and they live only through use (see *ibid.*, §546, §432), while his criticism of the Augustinian picture of language, according to which words name objects, sentences are combinations of such names, and ostensive definition (naming) is the fundamental link between language and the world (see *ibid.*, §1, §6, §19-§32, §49, §58-§60), is congruent with Marx's prioritization of verbs, as manifestations of doings, over names.

The third and last point of discussion regarding the views of Marx and Wittgenstein on language and consciousness is one that has in fact been constantly present, even if implicitly, in our above analysis of their everyday, social, and practical nature and is no other than that of their materiality. Marx's materialism is, of course, one of the most famous aspects of his broader philosophical outlook. In particular, and as far as language and consciousness are concerned, Marx follows a radically materialist approach to both, treating language as sensuous human activity and consciousness as interwoven with material activity and conditioned and/or determined by the mode of production of material life (see e.g. Marx, 1992, pp. 356, 425-26; Marx and Engels, 1998, pp. 42, 49). In a similar fashion, the later Wittgenstein approaches language/meaning and consciousness as spatial and temporal phenomena that are part of human natural history, while also criticizing their "ethereal" conception (see e.g. Wittgenstein, 1969, p. 47; 1981, §127, §287; 2001, §25, §108, §412-§427, §618). But it is at this point a possible divergence between Wittgenstein and Marx emerges, which has to do with the exact characteristics of Marx's materialism and, more specifically, with its (potential) scientist, reductivist, and (economically and historically) deterministic aspects. This, of course, has been a central point of debate throughout the development of Marx scholarship and

Marxist thought and is certainly too complex an issue to be properly discussed here. Suffice to say, while there are various remarks in Marx's writings – the (in)famous scheme regarding base (economic structure of society) and superstructure (forms of social consciousness) being a prime example – that may seem to exhibit scientistic, reductivist, and deterministic tendencies (see e.g. Marx, 1990, pp. 90-91, 927-30; 1992, pp. 424-28; 1993, p. 85-87; Marx and Engels, 1983, pp. 62-65; 1998, pp. 42, 45, 49-50; 2002, pp. 196, 233), there are, at the same time, many cases in which Marx clearly tries to distance his kind of materialism from such tendencies (see e.g. Marx, 1990, pp. 493-94, 783-84; 1991, pp. 953-70; 1992, pp. 108, 155-56, 174, 385, 393; 1993, pp. 85-87, 109, 460, 687, 832, 888; 1994a; Marx and Engels, 1998, pp. 43, 46, 48, 481; Shanin (ed.), 1983, pp. 98-126, 134-37). In any case, what is most interesting for our purposes is that Wittgenstein, who, apart from the various (meta)philosophical affinities with Marx highlighted above, was also at least sympathetic towards certain aspects of Marx's broader political outlook (see e.g. Moran, 1972; Rhees, 1981, pp. 219-31; Monk, 1991, pp. 343, 348-49, 423-24; McGuinness, 2002), was critical of those tendencies, which may well be potential as far as Marx's thought is concerned, but are definitely actual as far as certain types of Marxism are concerned. Thus, we find Wittgenstein criticizing not only the scientistic, reductivist, and deterministic conceptions of the base-superstructure scheme and the teleological and deterministic conception of history, but also the (allegedly) scientific forms of Marxism and their scientistic aspects in general (see Wittgenstein, 1993, p. 441; 1998, pp. 5, 69, 71; Rhees, 1981, pp. 222-23).

3. *Marx and Wittgenstein on (the production of) subjectivity*

The above discussion of the views of Marx and Wittgenstein on language and consciousness already highlights the basic aspects of their respective approaches to the issue of (the production of) subjectivity. For both Marx and Wittgenstein, the human subject is thoroughly social, practical – and that means also productive, in the broadest sense of the term and as opposed to the "contemplative stance" (see Lukács, 1971, p. 89) – material (and thus also corporeal), and produced on the plane of the mundane (as both immanence and everydayness). It is this conception of subjectivity that is crystallized in Marx's approach to human essence as the ensemble of social relations (see Marx, 1994a) and in Wittgenstein's delineation of an emdodied human subject that is constitutively embedded through praxis, that is, through practical sayings and doings, in a diversity of language games and forms of life.[5] Marx's and Wittgenstein's take on (the production of) subjectivity is of a dual character, exhibiting both negative (as critical) and positive (as affirmative) aspects. It exhibits negative (critical) aspects, because it rejects a certain picture of human subjectivity, that of an individual human subject which may well be surrounded by and interacting with its social and natural environment, but is in the end constitutively autonomous from it. But it also exhibits positive (affirmative) aspects, since it puts forward a different conception of human subjectivity, that of a human subject that is continuously both constituted by and constituting/ instituting its natural and social surroundings. What needs to be stressed is that the commitment to the idea of a socially produced (individual) subject does not entail the disappearance of human agency or autonomy. What actually disappears is their fixed and reified conception, which is substituted by an open and praxis-based conception of individual human agency and autonomy as conditioned on and by social/collective agency and autonomy. After all, Marx not only highlights aspects of human agency through his various discussions of class struggle, class consciousness, and living labour, but explicitly states that "circumstances are changed by men" and that "men make their own history" (Marx, 1994a, p. 99; 1994b, p. 188). As far as Wittgenstein is concerned, his approach to meaning as a matter of use and human praxis in the context of (social) language-games/ form(s) of life and that to rule-following as a practice and institution are just two of the various instances on which he highlights the (socially) self-instituting character of the human form(s) of life (see Wittgenstein, 2001, §18-§43, §189-§202, §584), while (individual) human innovativeness

---

5   It should be noted that this approach to subjectivity is characteristic of the later phase of both philosophers' thought. However, Marx and Wittgenstein engage with the issue of human subjectivity in their early writings too, with the (individual) human subject appearing in the early Marx as an instantiation/manifestation of a universal human essence/nature, of the (social) human "species-being", i.e. free conscious activity (see e.g. Marx, 1992, pp. 328-30) and in the early Wittgenstein as not part of the world, but only its limit, disengaged thus from any constitutive role as far as the relation between language and the world is concerned and allowing for the identification of solipsism with realism (see Wittgenstein 1922, §5.5421, §5.631-§5.641). The question of the relation of those early conceptions of subjectivity to Marx's and Wittgenstein's later ones and the broader question of the (dis)continuity between the early and the later phases of their thought have in fact constituted central themes in each scholarship, as we can see for example in the debates shaped by the publication of Althusser (2005) and Crary and Read (eds.) (2000) respectively.

and intentionality are not eradicated, but rather understood in a radical, constitutively social manner as always conditioned by and embedded in (socio-historical) human institutions (see e.g. Wittgenstein, 2001, §204, §337, §380).

What Marx and Wittgenstein criticize and reject through their praxis-based and radically social approach is the Cartesian model of subjectivity. This model, in its numerous instantiations and variations, has been a defining feature of modernity and for our purposes may be summarized in the commitment to the idea of a universal (as essence), rational, scientific, autonomous subject that is unified and constituted as such through thought and self-consciousness, with thought/consciousness located in the mind and the mind not only posited as the centre of the subject, but also as an entity separate from the body. In opposition to this picture, Marx and Wittgenstein set the background for a de-centred approach to the human subject – an approach that would be further developed by analytic post-foundationalism and continental post-structuralism – as being produced by and in, as well as being a proper part of, a larger social and natural environment. The human subject is no more centred around the (Cartesian) mind as a thinking substance, but is constituted in an embodied manner, through diverse human praxis, as indeed an assemblage, network, or apparatus of social relations – and that means also of institutions, practices, techniques, discourses, bodies of knowledge, language games, and forms of life. The broader sphere of the 'inner' (including the mind) does not, of course, disappear as such, but is clarified as not being (ontologically/ epistemologically) private, constitutively unconditioned by the 'outer', or an ethereal form of the material 'outer' trapped in or shelled by the body.[6] The source, so to speak, of subjectivity is not a reified, incorporeal, thing-like entity in the form of mind, consciousness, soul, psyche, spirit, ego, I, self, or subject (see e.g. Marx and Engels, 1998, pp. 36-51, 103-124, 259-318; Wittgenstein, 2001, §316-§362, §398-§427, §571-§628), neither a material thing in the form of the brain (see e.g. Wittgenstein, 2001, §143-§178, §412; 1980a, §903-§906)); there is no thing that is added to a body-object that transforms it into a body-subject. Rather, the production of a body-subject from a body-object is a matter of sayings and doings between human bodies, embedded in and conditioned by their social and physical environment, and that is one of the ways in which both Marx

---

6   As Schatzki puts it, the later Wittgenstein approaches the mind as conditions of
     life (how things are standing and going for people) expressed by bodily sayings
     and doings (see Schatzki, 1996, p. 22).

and Wittgenstein may be viewed as trying to overcome the traditional binary oppositions between mind and body, subject and object, inner and outer, and so on. It may be argued then that the materialist character of Marx's and Wittgenstein's approaches to language and consciousness is manifested as a shared resolute commitment to corporeality as far as the issue of subjectivity is concerned, as we can see, paradigmatically, in the central role that sensuous human activity and bodily needs, skills, powers, and potentialities play in Marx's outlook (see e.g. Marx, 1994a; Marx and Engels, 1998, pp. 36-51) and in the later Wittgenstein's engagement with verbal and non-verbal pain behavior as part of his critique of the idea of a private language (see Wittgenstein, 2001, §243-§315), with Wittgenstein's stance synopsized in his famous aphorism "The human body is the best picture of human soul" (*ibid.*, Part II p. 152). The body ceases to function as a barrier to the (direct) access of one's mind from the others, but is viewed instead as that which produces, expresses, and, in the end, constitutes the mind. At the same time, language, as a manifestation of sensuous human activity, is no more considered as serving a single purpose, namely, the conveyance of thoughts (see e.g. *ibid.*, §304, §501), but as also producing, expressing, and communicating feelings, sensations, and affects, unfolding, thus, as a form of diverse, sophisticated, self-instituted body behavior and as a proper part of human natural history (see *ibid.*, §23-§25, §243-§245). From such a perspective, not only language and meaning are viewed as fully corporeal in the form of gestures and facial expressions, sounds, and inscriptions and the human beings as body-subjects that collectively produce meaning, but also the body-subject is radically linguistified; it is through language, as practical (i.e., not contemplating) consciousness and praxis, that the human body becomes an individual subject. In other words, the (human) body-subjects collectively produce and institute language and meaning and at the same time are produced, as individual body-subjects, by and through them, with language, and the symbolic in general, emerging as a demonstration of continuous, collective, human self-institution.

One of the conclusions that can be drawn from the above discussion is that for both Marx and Wittgenstein the production of (individual) subjectivity is preconditioned on the existence of a *self-instituted* social formation – society, collectivity, community – and, thus, also on some kind of collective subjectivity.[7] In Marx's writings, collective subjectivity,

---

7   It should be stressed that the existence of collective subjectivity does not necessarily presuppose a collective subject, at least in the form of a Cartesian subject projected on a group conceived as a unified conglomeration of individuals.

always viewed through the prism of class struggle, takes various forms; for example, as social classes and their corresponding forms of class consciousness, e.g. the proletariat (as revolutionary subject) vs. the bourgeoisie (see Marx and Engels, 1998, pp. 58-65; 2002, pp. 197-98, 219, 231-39, 244), but also as social relations, e.g. (living) labour vs. capital (see Marx, 1993, pp. 171, 211, 264-66, 272, 295-301, 309-11, 323, 450-71, 585, 620-21, 746, 831-33). Furthermore, and most interestingly for the purposes of this essay, it also takes the cognate forms of the general intellect and social brain (general social knowledge and skills), as well as those of the social body and social subject (see *ibid.*, pp. 86, 694, 704-06, 832). In Wittgenstein's later writings, collective subjectivity may be viewed as manifested in our verbal and non-verbal practices (i.e., institutions, language games, etc.) and it can thus be considered as taking the shape of our – always materially and socio-historically produced and conditioned – form(s) of life in which these practices and institutions are embedded (see Wittgenstein, 1978, Part II §23, Part VI §32, Part VII §47; 1981, §534; 1998, p. 36; 2001, §7, §19, §23, §199, §240-§241, §337, §540, §584, Part II pp. 148, 192). It should be stressed that the concept of form(s) of life, as a concept that encompasses diverse manifestations of life – highlighting the amalgamation of the biological and the socio-historical aspects of human life – is constitutively elastic and indefinite (see Wittgenstein, 1980b, §652; 1998, p. 83; 1982, §206, §211, §246). It is these exact features of the Wittgensteinian conception of form(s) of life that may be viewed as key for the development of the distinctive Italian biopolitical approach to the general intellect. According to that approach, the general intellect is no more considered as just expressing the general state of science and technology objectified in fixed capital (see Marx 1993, pp. 699-712), but as indeed involved in the production of humans by means of humans, manifesting itself, as living labour, in our common verbal and non-verbal sayings and doings that articulate social communication, production, and life, and taking the shape of formal and informal knowledge and know-how, techniques, language games, epistemological paradigms, ethical tendencies, social imaginaries, worldviews, forms of conduct, and so on (see e.g. Hardt and Negri, 2000, pp. 27-30, 364-67; Negri, 2004, p. 361; Agamben, 1996, p. 154-155; Virno, 1996, pp. 20-24). This widened account of the general intellect and of its role as the main productive force (see Marx, 1993, p. 705) has in fact allowed for contemporary Italian radical

---

For more on this point see Foucault (1978, pp. 94-95) and Hardt and Negri (2004, pp. xiv-xv, 99-101, 105, 242-43, 328-31).

theory to analyze and criticize the new (post-1970s) forms of capitalist production, exploitation, and domination, as well as to highlight the new forms of class struggle and insurgent potentialities, with one of the main conclusions of that approach being the following. While the capitalist mode of production may be viewed as always having as its final result, in the long run and as a whole, the production of social life, of individual and collective subjectivities, of "the human being itself in its social relations" (*ibid.*, p. 712), in late capitalism, immaterial (as cognitive and affective) labour and biopolitical production (i.e., the production of social relations, subjectivities, and forms of life) are the hegemonic forms that the actual, *direct* process of the capitalist production of commodities and value takes.

4. *Late capitalism and Wittgensteinian biopolitics*

Within the diverse family of approaches shaped in the context and the aftermath of the *Operaismo* and *Autonomia* radical movements in the 1960s and 1970s that constitute contemporary Italian radical thought – from Negri's and Virno's engagement with the post-1970s transformations of capital, labour, and life and their emphasis on the transition from the hegemony of industrial labour to the hegemony of immaterial labour (i.e., the production of information, forms of knowledge, languages, ideas, symbols, codes, images, relationships, and affects),[8] to Agamben's reflections on 'bare life' and its (re)production by biopower and the sovereign state of exception – the fundamentally biopolitical character of late capitalism emerges as a shared topos. Biopolitical production, that is, the production of subjectivities, social relations, and forms of life, is identified as a constitutive characteristic of late capitalism, with the social relation of the common playing a central role in the relevant analyses. The use of the notion of the common in contemporary Italian radical theory may be viewed as an expression of both a philosophical approach influenced by Marx's and Wittgenstein's views on language, consciousness, and (the production of) subjectivity as discussed above and as based on a form of intersubjectivity that comes to replace the traditional philosophical dichotomies such as subject-object, identity-difference, universal-particular, public-private, etc., as well as a radical

---

8   Note that what is immaterial in immaterial labour is its products and not the labour process itself, which remains of course material, since it involves our brains and bodies (see Hardt and Negri 2004, pp. 108-09).

political approach based on a social relation antagonistic to some of the key capitalist ones, such as capital, value, and property (see e.g. Negri, 2004; Hardt and Negri, 2009, pp. vii-xiv, 107-28, 268-74; Virno, 2004, pp. 35-45, 66-71; Virno, 2015, pp. 221-36; Agamben, 2013, pp. xiii, 58-59, 71-72, 110-43; Agamben, 2016, pp. 80-94, 240-44). As a concept, it does not designate just the material commons (air, water, earth, etc.), but also the immaterial products of labour and the means of future production, with language constituting the site of the production *in* common and *of* the common par excellence (see e.g. Hardt and Negri, 2009, p. 121-22, 139; Negri, 2004, pp. 353-54; Virno, 2004, pp. 25-26, 35-45, 55-66, 76-84, 106-08; Virno, 2015, pp. 29-35, 64-68, 157-64, 175-86, 224-27; Agamben, 1996). The common constitutes, rather paradoxically, both a foundation and a result of a process, both a productive force and the form in which wealth is produced, it is both the object and the subject of production (see Hardt and Negri, 2009, pp. 119-37, 280-85). Furthermore, the social relation of the common may be viewed as both an actuality, as based on the cooperative, collaborative, and communicative character of immaterial and biopolitical production (see Hardt and Negri, 1994, pp. 275-83; 2009, pp. 153-64), and a potentiality, in the form of "making the common", that is, an ethico-socio-political project (see Hardt and Negri, 2004, pp. 103-15; 2009, pp. 112-37), as both an existing and a potential new way of relating to the products of our labour and the means of their production. Thus, the common emerges as both an epistemological-ontological given and a form of social praxis and process, a dynamic self-transforming and self-producing social relation. It is from such a perspective that the analysis and critique of contemporary, late capitalism stand in need not only of a new theory of value, but also of a new theory of subjectivity – new as compared to the traditional Marxist approaches – that focuses on language as a productive power (see Hardt and Negri, 2000, pp. 28-29; Virno, 2004, pp. 106-07), with Wittgenstein's later approach to subjectivity, as discussed above, being of crucial importance for its development. In fact, Negri not only holds that "continental philosophy would be unthinkable today without the Wittgensteinian heritage" and that "Wittgenstein, much more than Heidegger, was the one who enabled us to enter into the postmodern" (Negri and Dufourmantelle, 2004, pp. 176-77), but actually identifies, together with Hardt, a new theory of subjectivity, as also a critique of (traditional) epistemology, in what they call 'Wittgensteinian biopolitics' (see Hardt and Negri, 2009, pp. 121-28, 189-99).

While Hardt and Negri, as well as Agamben and Virno as we saw above, have highlighted certain aspects of Wittgensteinian biopolitics, the project of the development of a Wittgensteinian approach to the production of subjectivity in relation to late capitalism is far from complete. Let me just briefly sketch three points regarding its potential further development. The first point concerns the place and nature of reification in late capitalism. The question of the status of reification in the context of the hegemony of biopolitical production has not attracted much attention within Italian biopolitical theory.[9] Later Wittgenstein's critique of the reification of language and meaning, with meaning and language approached not as a thing or as a relation between things (words, objects, or logical forms), but as a social relation, or rather a network of social relations, as well as his critique of the reification of the inner, as discussed in the previous sections, may provide a fruitful point of departure for addressing that question. The second point deals with the notion of the multitude as the new collective revolutionary/political subject composed of a multiplicity of singularities and based not on some kind of (single) identity, but on the social relation of the common (see e.g. Hardt and Negri, 2004, pp. xiii-xv; Agamben, 1996; Virno, 2004, pp. 21-26). Wittgenstein's discussion of family resemblances as a kind of relation that designates not the sharing of a single common (set of) characteristic(s), but a network of overlapping similarities (see Wittgenstein, 2001, §65-§69) may highlight further the way in which singularities come together to form a multitude, not on the basis of identity, but of the overlapping characteristics they partially share in common, as well as the mutual, but asymmetrical, constitution of individual and collective subjectivity.[10] The third point has to do with the combinatorial import of the later Wittgenstein's criticisms of the idea of a private language (see Wittgenstein, 2001, §243-§315), especially in the form they take in the 'beetle in the box' thought experiment (*ibid.*, §293), and his remarks on the non-proprietary nature of subjective experience (*ibid.*, §398-§403). What these remarks highlight in fact is the non-proprietary character of (the production of) human subjectivity in general, especially in relation to language, the body, and the 'inner', and, hence, to the means and the products of immaterial and biopolitical production. It should also be noted that the above three points may not only contribute

---

9   Virno's idiosyncratic take on reification constitutes a notable exception (see Virno, 2015, pp. 135-168).

10   An image that could be of help regarding the relation between collective and individual subjectivity: collective subjectivity as a bowl of soup and individual subjectivity as a spoonful of soup (and as opposed to the image of collective subjectivity as a bowl of rice and individual subjectivity as a grain or spoonful of rice).

to the further theoretical development of Wittgensteinian biopolitics, but they have the potential to advance our engagement with certain concrete political issues characteristic of late capitalism too, such as the reification of the biopolitical productive powers, identity politics, and the struggles over intellectual property.

In this short essay we examined some of the views of Marx and the later Wittgenstein on language, consciousness, and (the production of) subjectivity that designate an ontology not centered around a "metaphysics of the subject", but conceived as "a fabric and product of collective praxis" (Negri, 2017, p. 197), as well as the relevance of those views for the analysis and critique of late capitalism as characterized by the hegemonic role of biopolitical production. Through this discussion, not only Marx, as Althusser has argued in his "anti-humanist" approach to Marx's (later) work (see Althusser, 2005, pp. 219-47), but Wittgenstein too emerge as forerunners of what Foucault has called, in reference to Nietzsche's work, the "death of man" (see Foucault, 2002, pp. 371-73), i.e., the demise of the anthropological engagement with man or human nature as a trans-historical essence.[11] But, of course, what the "death of man" signifies is the rejection of a certain cluster of approaches to human nature and subjectivity and not the absolute end of any reflection on the human condition. As Negri observes, in a manner consistent with his previous engagements with the concepts of anti-modernity/alter-modernity and anti-globalization/alter-globilization (see Hardt and Negri, 2009, pp. 102-03), the Marxist critique of the subject cannot be translated into some kind of non-qualified anti-humanism and thus a new kind of humanism is required (see Negri, 2017, pp. 197-98). For the development of such a kind of alter-humanism, the affirmative aspects of Wittgenstein's later views as discussed in this essay have the potential to play a crucial role.

References

Agamben, G. (2016). *The Use of Bodies*. Stanford: Stanford University Press.

Agamben, G. (2013). *The Highest Poverty: Monastic Rules and Form-of-Life*. Stanford: Stanford University Press.

---

11   For a detailed discussion of Wittgenstein's post-Cartesian conception of subjectivity and its relation to the debates over the "death of man" see Bax (2011).

Agamben, G. (1996). Form-of-Life. In P. Virno and M. Hardt (Eds.). *Radical Thought in Italy: A Potential Politics*. Minneapolis: University of Minnesota Press, pp. 150-56.

Althusser, L. (2005). *For Marx*. London: Verso.

Bax, C. (2011). *Subjectivity After Wittgenstein: The Post-Cartesian Subject and the "Death of Man"*. London: Continuum.

Crary, A. and Read, R. (Eds.). (2000). *The New Wittgenstein*. London: Routledge.

Foucault, M. (2002). *The Order of Things: An Archeology of the Human Sciences*. London: Routledge.

Foucault M. (1978). *History of Sexuality Volume I: An Introduction*. New York: Pantheon Books.

Hardt M. and Negri A. (2009). *Commonwealth*. Cambridge, MA: Harvard University Press.

Hardt M. and Negri A. (2004). *Multitude: War and Democracy in the Age of Empire*. New York: Penguin Press.

Hardt M. and Negri A. (2000). *Empire*. Cambridge, MA: Harvard University Press.

Lukács G. (1971). *History and Class Consciousness: Studies in Marxist Dialectics*. Cambridge: MIT Press.

Marx K. (1994a). Theses on Feuerbach. In *Selected Writings*. Indianapolis: Hackett, pp. 98-101.

Marx K. (1994b). The Eighteenth Brumaire of Louis Bonaparte (Selections). In *Selected Writings*. Indianapolis: Hackett, pp. 187-208.

Marx K. (1993). *Grundrisse*. London: Penguin.

Marx K. (1992). *Early Writings*. London: Penguin.

Marx K. (1991). *Capital Volume III*. London: Penguin.

Marx, K. (1990). *Capital Volume I*. London: Penguin.

Marx K. and Engels, F. (2002). *The Communist Manifesto*. London: Penguin.

Marx K. and Engels, F. (1998). *The German Ideology*. Amherst, NY: Prometheus Books.

Marx K. and Engels F. (1983). *Collected Works* Vol. 39, New York: International Publishers.

McGuinness B. (2002). It Will be Terrible Afterwards, Whoever Wins. In *Approaches to Wittgenstein: Collected Papers*. London: Routledge, pp. 43-52.

Monk R. (1991). *Ludwig Wittgenstein: The Duty of Genius*. London: Vintage.

Moran J. (1972). Wittgenstein and Russia. *New Left Review*, No. 73, pp. 85-96.

Negri A. (2017). Marx after Foucault: The Subject Refound. In *Marx and Foucault*, Cambridge: Polity Press, pp. 188-98.

Negri A. (2004). Wittgenstein and Pain: Sociological Consequences. *Genre*, Vol. 37, No. 3-4, pp. 353-67.

Negri A. and Dufourmantelle A. (2004). *Negri on Negri*. New York: Routledge.

Rhees R. (1981). Postscript. In R. Rhees (ed.) *Ludwig Wittgenstein: Personal Recollections*. Oxford: Blackwell, pp. 190-231.

Schatzki T. (1996). *Social Practices: A Wittgensteinian Approach to Human Activity and the Social*. Cambridge: Cambridge University Press.

Shanin T. (ed.) (1983). *Late Marx and the Russian Road*. New York: Monthly Review Press.

Virno P. (2015). *When the Word Becomes Flesh: Language and Human Nature*. South Pasadena: Semiotext(e).

Virno P. (2004). *A Grammar of the Multitude: For an Analysis of Contemporary Forms of Life*. Los Angeles: Semiotext(e).

Virno P. (1996). The Ambivalence of Disenchantment. In P. Virno and M. Hardt (eds.) *Radical Thought in Italy: A Potential Politics*. Minneapolis: University of Minnesota Press, pp.13-33.

Wittgenstein L. (2001). *Philosophical Investigations*. Oxford: Blackwell.

Wittgenstein L. (1998). *Culture and Value*. Oxford: Blackwell.

Wittgenstein L. (1993). Lectures on Freedom of the Will. In J. Klagge and A. Nordmann (Eds.) *Ludwig Wittgenstein: Philosophical Occasions 1912-1951*. Indianapolis: Hackett, pp. 427-44.

Wittgenstein L. (1982). *Last Writings on the Philosophy of Psychology* Vol. I. Oxford: Blackwell.

Wittgenstein L. (1981). *Zettel*. Oxford: Blackwell.

Wittgenstein L. (1980a). *Remarks on the Philosophy of Psychology* Vol. I. Oxford: Blackwell.

Wittgenstein L. (1980b). *Remarks on the Philosophy of Psychology* Vol. II. Oxford: Blackwell.

Wittgenstein L. (1978). *Remarks on the Foundations of Mathematics*. Oxford: Blackwell.

Wittgenstein L. (1969). *The Blue and Brown Books: Preliminary Studies for the 'Philosophical Investigations'*. Oxford: Blackwell.

Wittgenstein L. (1922). *Tractatus Logico-Philosophicus*. London: Routledge and Kegan Paul.

GUIDO SEDDONE

MARX AND WITTGENSTEIN ON THE TRUE NATURE OF HUMAN AGENCY

1. *Introduction*

Marx, in his attempt to revisit and renew political economy, addresses the classical economists of the eighteenth century and what he calls "physiocratic system" (Marx, 2011, p. 361) of economy and economic relations. Following this conception wealth is a natural product that should be understood by accounting for the natural conditions of goods' production like land, natural resources, agriculture, livestock, etc. Moreover, Marx acknowledges Adam Smith's merit of highlighting that a product in general is the general result of labor, namely of an activity and competence with social and normative requisites. However, Smith himself falls back into the "physiocratic system" when he explains labor as incapsulated into natural conditions like the presence of fruitful land and natural resources (*ibid.*, p. 362). The "physiocratic system" entails some methodological issues like the schematic description of the basic principles of economics such as production, exchange, distribution and consumption, and the abstract definition of their interconnection and interdependence. Marx's criticism specifically puts the focus on the abstract philosophical attitude of those economists to explain these basic principles regardless of the real and practical conditions of their development, conditions that should be instead traced back to the human and interpersonal activities. As a result of such attitude, they supply us with a less concrete exposition of human economy, which results schematic and based on dualism. Their schematic approach accounts for production, exchange, distribution and consumption as a linear process in which the starting point appears to be production, the final end is consumption, whereas exchange and distribution are supposed to represent the middle (*ibid.*, pp. 328-331). Marx rightly observes that this structure radical changes the relation between production and consumption, and consequently the human and social aspects connected to the economy. In fact, if we merely conceive of production as the process by which the person or the worker "is embodied in things", and of consumption as "things embodied in the persons" (*ibid.*, p. 329), we disregard the real nature of economy, which is the individual and social process of gaining some profit or benefit. In other words, when one overlooks the underlining factor of the economy one risks being victim of permanent confusion about the social and economic frame that guarantees wealth. Moreover, this misconception is increased by the fact that the linear description of the basic principles of economy looks correct although it entails many simplifications and superficialities. Following Marx, in contrast, the economic context is established by means of structural relations shaped by the concreteness of labor, goods, wealth and interests, which should not be taken for granted or overlooked because they represent the real essence of the productive weave. Therefore, political economy can only be modernize and become effective if we are able to understand the concrete reasons of the development of economic practices and if we can avoid any sort of justification of them by means of a self-justification of already existent setups, social compositions and eventually uneven distribution.

It is not a case at all, in fact, that the "physiocratic system" leads to the justification of the bourgeoise society, wrongly conceived as the natural development of given and natural economic patterns that the European society was able in a precise period of history to improve to its highest efficiency. This is the result of treating the connection between production, exchange, distribution and consumption as a procedural and mechanical chain of "events" that should contribute to social and individual wealth. This totally disregards the practical element and the way how human agency is shaped by means of the participation to the economic process. In contrast, Marx points out that understanding the social conditions in which any economic process takes place means explaining not only the concrete economic evolution, but also the reasons behind uneven distribution, social hegemony of some classes and conflicts based on economic injustice. In other words, Marx individuates the logical hidden thread that leads to the legitimation of the bourgeois society and that starts in the tiny wrinkles of the eighteenth century's economics. Following Marx, this legitimation is wrong because it is the result of seeing "the bourgeois in all forms of society" (*ibid.*, p. 365), whereas the specific conditions for the emergence of the modern European nations are not disclosed in the previous economic institutions, but they are rather the outcome of unique practical and intersubjective relations that are established in an unique way. In contrast, the classical economists of the eighteenth century relate the development of modern economy to abstract non-historical categories like tributes, taxes, wages, property, etc. that cannot be linked to the crucial factor that this development entails a radical mutation of both the human persons and the systems of production. In other words, they disregard the real practical circumstances of production and merely deal with regulative principles ruling production, distribution and consumption.

Marx's outlook is, in contrast, much wider because it aims at addressing how the concrete economic conditions have changed and what kind of impact they have on society. His main point is, of course, labor that, as he states, becomes in the modern era the most effective and valuable resource in favor of the human wealth. Labor is for him the meaning itself of the wealth of the nations and the bourgeois society has had the merit to boost its value and potentiality and to exploit it for sake of goods' production. Marx's explanatory strategy aims at disclosing and elucidating the concrete meaning of the productive practices by investigating the real conditions in which they are evolved and maintained. This approach reveals important affinities to Wittgenstein's thought about meaning, explanation and rule following that make possible, I believe, to understand what Marx was really seeking.

In other words, Wittgenstein's philosophy could be considered as an additional methodological tool we can use for addressing the crucial marxist concern about how practices and certainties are developed and why sometimes we are not able to completely figure out how misconceptions and fallacies about them arise. Although Wittgenstein's thought is centered on the idea that philosophy "leaves everything as it is" (*PI* §124) and this contradicts marxist proposal to change the world by revolutionizing the social relations, the Austrian philosopher also introduced the idea of philosophy as a discipline that corrects conceptual confusions about the grammar of our practices. Therefore, it is not totally correct to state that Wittgenstein's philosophy represents a renounce of every kind of philosophical activity, it is rather more correct to acknowledge its role as a therapy of our language and its use. Hence, we should read the following passages from *Zettel* as complementary and not contradictory:

> 450. One who philosophizes often makes the wrong, inappropriate gestures for a verbal expression.

> 452. How does it come about that philosophy is so complicated a structure? It surely ought to be completely simple, if it is the ultimate thing, independent of all experience, that you make it out to be. — Philosophy unties knots in our thinking; hence its result must be simple, but philosophizing has to be as complicated as the knots it unties.

The first paragraph points out the classical philosophical mistake of being inappropriate as compared to the practices and their grammar, which is solidified by means of the uses and the spontaneous agreement about the linguistic games. The second one, instead, highlights that philosophy as the ultimate thing "unties knots in our thinking", namely resolves problems and confusions that can develop within the grammar itself. Wittgenstein teaches us an important lesson about philosophy when he states that it can generate problems when it disregards the concrete grammar of the practices. However, another important lesson is also that philosophical task consists in discovering disorders created by other philosophers in their attempt to produce abstract theories about the meaning and the sense of our practical life. Since philosophy is not the only source of grammatical confusions, its role is to trace back every explanation to the practical sphere of the uses, because this is the appropriate way to understand the grammar of our linguistic games and forms of life. Since "the philosopher is not a citizen of any community of ideas" (*Z* §455), his role is to point out that there is no extra grammatical normativity governing our language and that every rule following is a social matter.[1] This aspect is the first comparison I intend to make with Marx's thought, because he also stresses the importance of explaining any social and economic phenomenon by avoiding schematic descriptions and by focusing on the intra-normative conditions through which every productive interconnection is established (what Wittgenstein would call the grammar of a form a life). For him it is also of primary importance to assume the agents' perspective in order to clear the reasons of the economic course of a civilization, rather to conceive of the human activities as procedural events. Like Wittgenstein, he is aware that the grammar operates as an internal and evolving condition of the human activities and that misconceptions and confusions originates in schematic descriptions and categorizations of it. Finally, he also warns from the risk of establishing hegemonic interpretations and theories about the practical

---

1   Wittgenstein *PI*, § 200: "It is, of course, imaginable that two people belonging to a tribe unacquainted with games should sit at a chess-board and go through the moves of a game of chess; and even with all the appropriate mental accompaniments. And if $n>e$ were to see it we should say they were playing chess. But now imagine a game of chess translated according to certain rules into a series of actions which we do not ordinarily associate with a *game*—say into yells and stamping of feet. And now suppose those two people to yell and stamp instead of play- ing the form of chess that we are used to; and this in such a way that their procedure is translatable by suitable rules into a game of chess. Should we still be inclined to say they were playing a game? What right would one have to say so?"

sphere that degenerate into the legitimation of dominant classes, labor exploitation and uneven distribution of wealth.

In this contribution I intend to tackle the connection between Marx's and Wittgenstein's thoughts from the point of view of their conception of social practices, explanation, meaning and use and to highlight that both thinkers aim at transforming the role of philosophy into an instrument for the diagnosis of human organization of the communitarian and productive life. I will firstly give an account of Marx's conception about the relation between labor and production and I will highlight that the former represents for him the concrete practical meaning through which one should explain both social and individual wealth. Secondly, I will emphasize that Wittgenstein also conceives of the meaning as something that can be explained through its use and the human person cannot be estranged by her rule following. Eventually, I will defend the idea that for both Marx and Wittgenstein enormous confusions and misconceptions arise when one disregards this concrete practical dimension, which jeopardize the philosophical task to account for the real conditions under which the practical life is set up.

2. *Marx on the concrete meaning of wealth*

In Marx's philosophy there is a central issue that characterizes his speculation about society, politics and economics and that can be interpreted from a Wittgensteinian perspective, namely the effort to pinpoint what I call *the concrete meaning of wealth and production*. In fact, although it is quite ascertained that economics deals with the question about the wealth of the nations and societies, no philosopher like and before Marx tried to investigate with the same precision and meticulousness the concrete and effective source of goods' production. As we mentioned before, the eighteenth century economists completely disregard this point and schematically describe wealth as the result of the linear sequence of production, exchange, distribution and consumption and, moreover, they also linked production prevalently to the presence of natural resources. Marx intends to change this approach and points out that wealth is a social fact concretely connected to social and historical conditions that should be tackled and understood holistically. Therefore, one should avoid to treat the above mentioned principles in a linear and schematic way and should instead consider them as tightly connected. This means firstly reorganizing the notion itself of production by considering it not just as the consequence of consumption, but rather as what determines consumption itself. Marx

(2011, pp. 328-352) for the first time underlines that consumption like exchange and distribution are not extra economic aspects of economy, namely phenomena resulting from economy, they are rather economics itself because they integrally contribute to the determination of wealth, individual interests and instruments of production. Eighteenth century's economists in their "shallow conception" (Marx, 1859, p. 345) usually treat production as a natural fact and as an "eternal truth" (*ibid.*, p. 346), and distribution as a legal question that can be historically established. This approach displays its abstractness because distribution determines production to the extent that the latter depends on the diffusion of certain instruments of production like machinery, competencies, education, skills and even capital, which is also an instrument for boosting productivity (*ibid.*, p. 341). Marx like Ricardo claims that distribution pertains to the domain of economics rather than to the domain of law, and also demonstrates the interdependence of these basic principles of wealth. A similar approach he has towards consumption, which is normally conceived as what determines production because of the simple argument that the consumer decides her own wants and wishes. Marx instead underlines that consumption and production have a reciprocal dependence since one can consume what is produced and brought to the markets. This point of view implies the very important notion that the economy is developed by also determining the behaviours and the wants of the consumers of the goods and finalized products, what enhances our understanding about the impact of the economy in our practical life. By explaining the connection between those principles of the economy Marx radically changes our comprehension about the wealth and economic practices. In fact, rather than conceiving of productivity as a natural fact independent from other more sociological aspects he links it to the latter, what has three major philosophical outcomes.

The first is to abandon the abstruse idea that he defines as "Robinsonades" (*ibid.*, p. 317) that production is natural because human beings have always produced something from the age of the hunters and gatherers till modern times. He instead teaches us that production in the bourgeoisie society has assumed specific and unique characteristics that one should address and issue in order to figure out its impacts on societies, workers and citizens. Such features can be correctly tackled only if one is able to grasp the complex net of human relations, duties, needs, wants, interests, etc. that are at the bottom of enormous growth of productivity, technology, labor division, financial aspects, capital concentration, etc. The second outcome is the possibility to finally highlight that behind social and individual wealth there are individual persons, competencies, skills, needs, relations, contexts, in one word a practical dimension at whose bottom stands labor as the ultimate source of wealth. Eventually, both the complexities and the problems of the social relations connected to productivity can be addressed because economy can be finally conceived as a social and collective enterprise. In other words, every stage of society and goods' production, distribution and consumption can be considered as involved in wealth (both individual and common). As a consequence, also the social problems like work exploitation, low wages, uneven distribution, control of instruments of production, concentration of capital, etc. can be issued and explained by making recourse to this wider notion of political economy.

Differently from the schematic separation of production from distribution and consumption, Marx's conception makes us able to consider both economy and wealth as the outcomes of social and practical requisites that do not exclusively pertain to the productive domain, but rather to every domain connected to wares, goods, interests, investments, etc. He teaches us that the economic course and the related social effects are shaped by means of the influence of a net of practical conditions through which the wealth of a nation is created and distributed. The ultimate social element that stands at the bottom of this net is, of course, labor because of its twofold character of being a social requisite and the instrument itself of productivity. Therefore, productivity is no natural activity for two reasons: 1) it is tightly bounded to several social activities like distribution, consumption and exchange and cannot be understood out of the practical frame of human occupations; 2) it is the outcome of individual work which is related to competencies and skills that are socially acquired, acknowledged and recompensed. Following Marx, labor is the primary source of wealth and the economic disciplines should explain every aspects of productivity by giving an account of it. Every aspect of the economic life is centered on labor, even its exploitation and low wages, because controlling it is like controlling the wellspring of prosperity and opulence.

Marx's great merit is having highlighted that explaining wealth requires a perspicuous analysis of the practical dimension in which it is created, distributed and consumed and that each phase of the economic process is linked to the other in a circular way so that they are reciprocally influenced. Every attempt to clear economy that takes this fact for granted seriously risks a schematic approach leading to a linear conception in which the concrete sphere of human activities results disregarded. His approach is strongly devoted to the idea that misconceptions about the concrete structure of economy can possibly foster both the establishment of individual interests over common ones and hegemonic attitudes and privileges of some classes.

Tracing back production to its concrete practical and relational conditions makes us able to understand economy as a shared enterprise whose authenticity is represented by labor as the definitive source of the wares and the social wealth.

3. *Wittgenstein on meaning, explanation and rule following*

The previous paragraph about Marx and the productive practices indicates that this philosopher conceives of the economy as a discipline that should investigate the concrete relationships and links between agents, interests and methods of production. His aim is to eschew any schematic elaboration of the economic matter and to highlight that the concrete sense of wealth is social and based on shared practices and interpersonal relations. Production, distribution and consumption, for instance, contribute jointly to determine wealth and the direction of the economic progress, whereas treating them separately would jeopardize the possibility of binding the historical course of economy to the social practices involved in it. Thus, exploitation of workers and low wages are the result of a dominant vision on production that ignores the fact that labor is the ultimate source and meaning of wealth and that any political economy should issue this fact.

Wittgenstein's thought does not have any explicit reference to economy, nonetheless his thinking contributes to enhance our understanding about the practical dimension and about the confusions and misconceptions arising from a wrong approach. Like Marx, he claims that we cannot clear the meaning of a practice through a mere ostensive explanation because this would undermine our possibility to understand how it is connected to a form of life. Both the practices and the language are free-floating structures that are not connected to a reality empirically conceived, they are rather to be grasped in terms of forms of life shared and socially acknowledged.[2] The following passage from the *Philosophical Investigations* clearly unfolds what Wittgenstein means for agreement:

---

2   Wittgenstein *PI*, § 23: "But how many kinds of sentence are there? Say assertion, question, and command?—There are *countless* kinds: countless different kinds of use of what we call 'symbols', 'words', 'sentences'. And this multiplicity is not something fixed, given once for all; but new types of language, new language-games, as we may say, come into existence, and others become obsolete and get forgotten. (We can get a *rough picture* of this from the changes in mathematics.) Here the term '*language-game*' is meant to bring into prominence the fact that the *speaking* of language is part of an activity, or of a form of life."

"So you are saying that human agreement decides what is true and what is false?" — It is what human beings say that is true and false; and they agree in the language they use. That is not agreement in opinions but in form of life. (*PI*, § 241)

The agreement in *form of life* is the main factor deciding the correctness of our practices and any philosophical attempts to evaluate them from an external and observational outlook will fail because it would disregard their fluid and fluctuating feature. The probably primary lesson Wittgenstein intends to teach us in the *Philosophical Investigations* by condemning the ostensive explanation is to assume a participant perspective in order not to miss the ramifications and spontaneous expansion of the human activities. In fact, the ostensive explanation entails a schematic and reduced interpretation of the human linguistic games because it is extra-practical and based on truth-conditions.

For Wittgenstein, instead, the grammar of the human forms of life is autonomous because it is set up from within and its correctness is decided by the participants themselves. Therefore, any explanation of the meaning is a question of a training to use a word or to follow a rule in the respective context and it is not a question of its universal reference, because this does simply not exist except in the mind of the philosophers. This model of explanation can be extended to the practices, which one is able to perform because of one's own integration to the linked intersubjective social activities. The passages of the *Philosophical Investigations* about rule following clearly highlight that belonging to a practice requires a sort of blindness (*PI*, § 219) about the practice itself because it represents the limit of one's own operational domain. This is the result of the non-ostensive conception of language that implies the idea that once educated to following patterns of activities we loose the need of the universal perspective that the ostensive approach fails to reach anyway. The agents are, hence, like embedded into "a series of rails invisibly laid to infinity" (*PI*, § 218) that "correspond to the unlimited application of a rule" (*PI*, § 218) and they are not able to reach a privileged perspective on them, since such perspective would compromise the comprehension of the free-floating nature of the human social practices and the possibility to keep belonging to them. In order words, the attempt itself to gain an ostensive description of a practice would mean abandoning it, since it would try to explain it in terms of truth conditions.

Wittgenstein's awareness about this point is almost obsessive because he also negates the possibility of a definitive justification for one's own following a rule in the famous aphorism about justification like a spade that gets turned when it reaches the bedrock (*PI*, § 217).[3] With this metaphor he wants to underline the stratification of human activities and the fact that we are not able to have an exhaustive and definitive comprehension about them because the certainties of the community are so branched out that our thinking is not able to contain them. Wittgenstein's contribution offers an interesting outlook about the intra-normative ramification of our practices and the way how they are interlinked. Human activities and individual competencies are shaped by means of such interconnection and many misconceptions would arise once we failed to acknowledge this fact.

I believe that Wittgenstein's notions of certainty and grammar as two intra-normative elements constituting our social practices are very close to Marx's conception about social and economic wealth. In fact, both certainty and wealth are evolved by anyone's contribution and both represent the core respectively of the former's notion of form of life and the latter's notion of economy. Following Marx wealth is the result of a complex network of activities and cannot be reduced to the production of natural goods because it is a social fact in which social acceptance, distribution and consumption play a main role for the determination of the value of the wares. Likewise, following Wittgenstein the agents establish the normative frame into which their own practices and certainties are organized and developed. The grammar of our human forms of life is intra-normative because every agent contributes to its definition, therefore no bird's eye view on them is properly possible. Wittgenstein's conception of following a rule supplies us with a straightforward definition of social practices that he considers as the limit itself of everyone's activities and the delimitation of everyone's set of skills and competencies. Although a rule is not rigid because there is a rule even when one breaks a rule (*PI*, § 201), clearly belonging to a community requires being master of procedures, norms, customs, uses and institutions (*PI*, § 199). The inseparable nature of belongingness and mastery of techniques represents both the limit and the extension of one's own practical domain and also of a community's tradition and historical identity.

---

3   Wittgenstein *PI*, § 217: " 'How am I able to obey a rule?'— if this is not a question about causes, then it is about the justification for my following the rule in the way I do. If I have exhausted the justifications I have reached bedrock, and my spade is turned. Then I am inclined to say: 'This is simply what I do.' "

4. *The role of philosophy*

For Wittgenstein it is very important to be aware of the numerous paths of the language (*PI*, § 203)[4] because the grammar of our behaviors and certainties is built on such ramification of uses and procedures. Any schematic explanation of these paths would reduce our capacity to analyze the social practices and to understand how humans jointly develop them by means of a spontaneous agreement in form of life and not in opinions (*PI*, § 241). Acknowledging this kind of organization is very important because it makes us able to understand its historic and contingent character that could not be grasped by means of an accurate representation based on truth-conditionals. It is instead necessary to understand the multiple variables of every discourse about the forms of life and to grasp them as the outcome of the participants' endorsement over them. Any intellectual attempt to overlook this approach would inexorably lead to an abstract and surreal vision about the human social activities that does not account for the concrete relationship between a practice and its participants and how they both determine each other. Following Wittgenstein, any investigation about language, rules, intersubjectivity and practical domain should address the constitutive aspect represented by the everyone's spontaneous contribution to shaping the practical dimension in which everyone is also immersed. This element is beneath the surface of human doings and stands for the identity of the community that, as we saw, Wittgenstein defines as "agreement in form of life" (*PI*, § 241). The philosopher should address this kind of agreement by eschewing any form of abstract categorization of human customs and uses and by giving an account of how linguistic games human interpersonal relations are threaded together.

Wittgenstein's concerns about traditional philosophy that does not acknowledge the concrete and fluid nature of the intra-normative grammar of human agency signify the expectation for a new philosophical approach that concentrates on its pragmatic conditions as the only ones that make us able to understand it. The role of the philosopher is, hence, to deconstruct philosophy itself and to supply us with a straightforward strategy of acknowledging the living, social and historical weaves from which the human existence, taste, experience and values are established.

---

4   Wittgenstein *PI*, § 203: "Language is a labyrinth of paths. You approach from *one* side and know your way about; you approach the same place from another side and no longer know your way about."

Marx and Marxism in general also conceive of this act of acknowledging as the necessary step towards a revision of society because the alteration of the real conditions of goods' production and distribution is due to a failed recognition of how human productive activities are organized. The possibility of exploitation and concentration of wealth is, in fact, linked to an established philosophical approach denying that misconceptions and confusions originate in a partial and abstract description of the conditions of labor and production. Gramsci's work, for instance, is an extraordinary example how Marxism and Wittgenstein's philosophy can match as he points out the necessity to enhance our understanding of how the cultural, pragmatical and economic aspects of society are interwoven in order to change the economic burdensome conditions of the workers and subalterns. Following Marx, there is a clear connection between the misconceptions of schematic methodology in economics and uneven distribution, low wages and work exploitation because these phenomena originate in the idea that economy is bare wares' production. Such approach disregards the fact the modern economy is much more articulated since it is also the result of methods of production, competencies and the capacity to coordinate the work of many employees. Because of this articulation the modern economists often undervalue that the concrete source of wealth is labor, namely the personal capacity to transform materials to goods and to distribute them. Work exploitation is the outcome of conceiving of wealth as merely related to productivity and to the presence of natural resources, whereas the concrete resource is everyone's capacity to transform them (Marx, 1859, pp. 82, 98). Marx clearly states the necessity to deal with labor as the core of economics and productivity because only this can emphasize the concrete structure of the society by eschewing any sort of misconception overshadowing the contribution of every worker to the productive practice. Marx's philosophy aims, hence, at restoring an authentic understanding of economics and productive systems in order to bring wealth back to its real source, namely labor and workers.

Wittgenstein's idea of philosophy is empathetic with Marx's one as he highlights the importance to acknowledge that human practices and languages are developed through a scheme relying on the intersection between rule following and belongingness to a community. Since rules are not fixed procedures, but they are rather established by the participants of a practice in order to agree through a form of life (*PI*, § 241), social activities cannot be explained by means of an abstract description that does not account for this mutual agreement, which is the basis of the practical dimension itself. Wittgenstein, thus, also pinpoints the concrete source of human practices and claims that they are fluid and contingent because of the spontaneous nature of human beings to agree on potentially infinite activities. In other words, behind every behaviour and action there is the social acknowledgement of everyone's role and task that can be grasped in terms of rule following. However, rule following is not the result of someone else dictating precise duties, but rather the outcome of activities mutually recognized. Overlooking this structure entails the risk of misconceiving the real existence of the practices and their members and to attain an alterate understanding of both. This is what also Marx maintains when he claims the necessity to understand the economic and productive process as a domain in which every aspect is integrated in order to supply its participants with wealth and goods. Overlooking the interdependence of production, distribution and labor would mean loosing the critical apparatus necessary to eschew the risk of labor exploitation and profit through low wages. In other words, following Marx, we can achieve human emancipation from material and economic burdensomeness only if we acknowledge that economy is not a question of production from nature, but rather a social fact composed of several aspects that are interdependent and holistically related. Only in this way we would be able to understand every underlying phenomenon connected to wealth that transforms economy from being a social matter into a question of individual interest and profit. The possibility itself of dissolving egoistic profitability relies on our philosophical explanation of economy as communitarian enterprise based on labor as the only concrete source of both individual and social wealth.

5. *Conclusion*

Marx and Wittgenstein express often a sincere concern about the misconceptions and confusions arising from a schematic and abstract explanation of the social and practical dimension of human beings. Although their interests and topics differ because the latter mostly addresses the nature of human practical agency in general, whereas the former puts the focus especially on the economy, we can state that there are compelling affinities about the way how they deal with this matter. Marx's deconstruction of previous economics aims at innovating political economy as a discipline that should address production and distribution from the point of view of labor as the primary source of wealth. Wittgenstein's practical philosophy is more devoted to explain the shape of human practices out of the spontaneity and belongingness of their participants. However, both agree that disregarding the true source of human agency is misleading because it leads us to miss connections, relations, interdependences, conditions, etc. that represent the historical and versatile nature of human doings and human cooperation. The comparison between Marx and Wittgenstein does not look at once as plausible because of the different targets of their respective philosophies. Nonetheless, a more thorough analysis points out that their reflections are complementary because they both understand human practical domain as an issue requiring a meticulous investigation due to its original complexity. In fact, they teach us that the development of the practices is very multifaceted because of the spontaneity of their members and no quick analysis would be ever able to provide a satisfying comprehension of them. Only dealing with the concrete and contingent system of interpersonal and normative frames of the forms of life may foster an effective understanding of the social sphere that will improve the role of the philosopher to furnish a helpful contribution to the progress of humanity.

References

Baker G. P. and Hacker P. M. S. (2005). *Wittgenstein: Understanding and Meaning* Part I. Malden (MA): Blackwell Publishing.
Marx K. (2011). *A Contribution to the Critique of Political Economy*. New York: Barnes & Noble, Inc.
Wittgenstein L. (1958). *Philosophical Investigations*. Oxford: Basil Blackwell. Abbreviated as *PI*.
Wittgenstein L. (1967). *Zettel*. Berkeley and Los Angeles (CA): Basil Blackwell. Abbreviated as *Z*.
Wittgenstein L. (1968) *On Certainty*. Oxford: Basil Blackwell. Abbreviated as *oC*.
Wittgenstein L. (1974). *Philosophical Grammar*. Oxford: Basil Blackwell. Abbreviated as *pG*.

CHRISTOPH DEMMERLING

REIFICATION: FROM MARX TO WITTGENSTEIN?[1]

1. *Introduction*

The concept of reification belongs among the central concepts of Marxist-influenced philosophy and social theory in the broadest sense. The expression gained its central contours as a concept of philosophical analysis and a historical diagnosis of the times in the 1920s by way of Lukács' now-legendary contribution *Reification and the Consciousness of the Proletariat* in his 1923 book *History and Class Consciousness*. Especially within critical theory, the term has been interpreted and reinterpreted in a variety of ways. Time and time again the question has been raised as to whether it, as a fundamental concept of historical diagnosis, can describe the self-understanding of people and their social relationships in modern capitalist societies.[2] It was authors like Marx, Weber and Simmel, on whose analyses Lukács relied to establish the concept of reification as a basic concept of a critical analysis of capitalism, and further, to establish a form of rationality corresponding to it. Criticism of modern capitalist society and criticism of philosophy, that is, of a particular form of a widespread concept of reason in philosophy, became closely linked. In practical terms, it was the experiences of the Weimar Republic, its political and economic crises, the disintegration of shared horizons of value and rampant unemployment, but also revolutionary hopes in relation to a transformation of the capitalist mode of production and its associated living conditions that shaped the background of Lukács' reflections. The theoretical outlook in philosophy

---

1   The reflections in this essay are partly based on sections of my book Demmerling (1994), as well as parts of my essays Demmerling (2014) and Demmerling (2018).
2   There are a number of different newer perspectives on Lukács, some of which try to modify his proposal but also distance themselves from some of its basic assumptions, for instance, Honneth (2005) and Quadflieg (2019). For the more recent discussion on the theory of reification in Lukács, see also the contributions in Gandesha & Hartle (2017).

as well as in relevant related disciplines such as sociology, but also the practical and social situation, had changed markedly in the hundred years since the publication of Lukács' text. Big concepts and big theories were no longer in good standing in view of small-scale forms of argumentation and differentiated special discussions which – and rightly so, one must add – prevailed more and more to the detriment of worldview influenced theoretical formats. Additionally, a revolutionary subject like the proletariat, which could for Lukács be united by way of all-encompassing and precarious living conditions, cannot be so easily identified today. Conditions have become less clear and the interests of people living in precarious conditions seem too heterogenous to be combined together by a single force on the basis of which social upheaval of whatever kind would in any case be but a faint premonition. Against this background of broadly outlined developments, can the concept of reification and its accompanying connotations still be taken up today? This is the question that I will pursue in this article.

In the first part I outline the meaning and the theoretical context of the concept of reification in Marx. Although he only uses the term sporadically, his reflections nonetheless provided the crucial impulses for Lukács' reification theory (I). The second part of the article takes a brief look at Lukács (II) before expanding on economic or rational-theoretical articulations of the analysis of reification to include a language-philosophical, or more precisely, language-critical dimension, which I elaborate by way of a reading of Wittgenstein (III).

2. *Alienation and Reification*

Central to Marx's use of reification is first and foremost his understanding of human labor, as developed in his early writings and primarily in reference to Hegel. In the *Paris Manuscripts*, labor is interpreted as a form or process of objectification. The conclusion of every work activity has, as its goal, objects that can be regarded as realizations of human purposes. One can think of manual, but also of industrial production. Products such as furniture or technical devices are manufactured according to specific ideas in order to fulfill a specific purpose. In this sense, it can be said that a cabinet as the result of carpentry work or a kitchen appliance as the result of an industrial production process represent a human purpose whose form has become an object. The process that leads from determining a purpose to the object can be described in a very literal sense as objectification. That which applies to objects in the narrower sense also applies to objects in a broader sense. The establishment of an institution or the establishment of a custom, though not objects in the narrower sense, can be described as an objectification of human purposes whether the latter consistently materialize or not. All products of human practice in which mental activities manifest can be viewed as objectifications.

The concept of objectification is used by Marx in a neutral way and in a manner different from the concept of *Verdinglichung*, which he uses later, on occasion (see Marx, 1964, pp. 838, 887). It is an anthropological fact that humans generate products by means of their abilities and actions, that they are able to materialize their ideas and purposes into practices, which, as such, need not be subject to critique. It is a part of human life that it externalizes itself and becomes object or quasi-objective, whether through labor, through other actions, or by way of language. But the young Marx already sees a problem in the fact that the products of human activity can completely detach themselves from their originators and begin to lead a life of their own. Central for him, first of all, is the sphere of labor. When, for instance, the entities produced by work can no longer be experienced as products of one's own activity, Marx speaks of alienation or alienated labor. Let's take a closer look at the issue in order to say something about reification on this basis.

Marx sees the core of all relations of alienation or rather of all forms of alienation in the alienation of the worker from the product of their activity under the conditions of capital relations of production. The existence of private property as well as the prevalence of the division of labor can be regarded as the decisive conditions of these relations. Under these conditions, according to Marx, products are no longer experienced as the results of the activity of the workers but are encountered by them as "*power independent*" (Marx, 2010, p. 272) which leads to a "*loss of realisation* for the workers", and then to alienation or – as the English translation reads – to "*estrangement*" (see, *ibid.*, pp. 272f.). The products produced through labor are no longer experienced as something that one has produced and that belongs to oneself. Taking his point of departure from alienated labor, Marx turns to other aspects of the issue of alienation. Since he conceives of history as a "creation of man through human labour, nothing but the emergence of nature for man", (*ibid.*, p. 305) he can characterize the entire relationship of man to the world as alienated. The alienated relationship of the worker to the products of his labor is "at the same time the relation to the sensuous external world, to the objects of nature, as an alien world inimically opposed to him" (*ibid.*, p. 275). In addition to the alienation of the worker from the products of his activity and the alienation of man from the world, Marx discusses the alienation of man from his own activity, which is also termed "*self-estrangement*" (*ibid.*). Under the conditions of capitalist relations of production workers can no longer classify their activity as an action in which their determined purposes materialize in a free way. The worker "therefore only feels himself outside his work, and in his work feels outside himself" (*ibid.*, p. 274). Finally, he discusses the alienation of man from the human species. This is not the place to address the many alienation phenomena differentiated by Marx and their relationship to each other in greater detail. It is however crucial that alienation is seen as something that is possible on the basis of objectification and which occurs once people no longer conceive of the products of their actions as such and these products begin to lead a life of their own. It is this thought, also in the context of Marx's writings on reification, which plays an especially important role.

This can be made clear by way of a brief look at Marx's reflections on the form of commodities and his analysis of commodity fetishism. Marx notices that the commodity is "a very queer thing abounding in metaphysical subleties and theological niceties" (Marx, 2010a, p. 81). Without going into detail on Marx's reflections on commodities, it can be said that commodities receive their form and value through human labor, which is then obscured in the end result. Social relationships are reinterpreted to become natural characteristics of things, taking on „the fantastic form of a relation between things" (*ibid.*, p. 83). This process can already be described as reification. With his analysis of commodity fetishism Marx believed to have found the place where reification originates. The creations of the human world are no longer conceived of as the products of human activity but rather as independent things, which in turn assume a controlling function and make people appear powerless. For Marx, the distinction between use value and exchange value is decisive in this context. The value of a product is primarily understood as its exchange value. In order to be able to exchange goods, they must be equivalent to one another in some way. If one follows Marx, objects become commodities insofar as the working time associated with them is taken to be the relevant variable and fundamentally different labor tasks are seen as equivalent in view of their equivalent time requirements, resulting in the value of a commodity. The fetishistic character of the commodity consists in the fact that its value appears as a natural property of the thing in question. Marx uses the fetish theorem, much like the concept of alienated labor in his early writings, to criticize capitalist relations of production by means of which the social origin of commodities is obscured. He also criticizes economic theories that make no contribution to clarifying the matter, but rather regard commodities and their value as nature-given. According to Marx, the economists "are misled by the Fetishism inherent in commodities, or by the objective appearance of the social characteristics of labour" (*ibid.*, p. 93). Further still: They not only succumb to the impression of appearances but contribute to its consolidation by acting as if the "forms of social life" belong to the "stability of natural [...] forms" (*ibid.*, p. 86, 93). The commodity appears as nature, and so something social gets represented as something natural. The value of things as commodities, which have social origins, appears as a natural property. Things, in this way, seem to become actors. Personal relationships appear thing-like. In this context, the expression and phenomenon of reification become relevant.

Marx never presented a fully developed theory of reification and his reflections are not always as clear as could be desired. In *Capital*, Marx speaks of a "conversion of social relations into things" (Marx, 2010b, p. 817), and, in German, of a "Verdinglichung der gesellschaftlichen Verhältnisse" (Marx, 1964, p. 838). He also speaks of an "objectification of the social features of production" (Marx, 2010b, p. 867). At this point, the German text reads: "Verdinglichung der gesellschaftlichen Produktionsbestimmungen" (Marx, 1964, p. 887). On the basis of the text, one can generally say at least this much: Reification is something that is related to the conditions of production; societal relationships take on the character of material, natural relationships. Something that humans have done appears as something independent from them and confronts them with a life of its own. Marx relates his reflections primarily to the transformation of objects that have a use value to commodities with an exchange value. There is much controversy surrounding Marx's analyses of commodity fetishism. For my purposes, only the idea that societal, social relationships between people appear as relationships between things, that this is consolidated within the framework of certain (economic) theories, and that the demonstrated objectification or reification has negative effects on people's living conditions is important.

3. *The Reification of Consciousness*

It is Marx's reflections on the transformation of relationships between people into relationships between things that Georg Lukács takes up in order to formulate a comprehensive conception of reification. It was through the work of Lukács that the concept of reification first turned into a fundamental concept of critical social philosophy. He expands Marx's conception of the reification of the form of the commodity and uses the expression in order to analyze all the expressions of life and habits of thought of a society. Within the history of the theory of Marxism, the work of Lukács leads to the universalization of the reification theorem. Let us consider the decisive theoretical choices that Lukács makes.

In his text *Die Verdinglichung und das Bewusstsein des Proletariats,* Lukács fuses Marx's critique of political economy and Max Weber's theory of rationalization together.[3] It is this connection that allows him to expand the concept of reification further than Marx's analysis of the commodity, using it as a multi-layered instrument for describing and criticizing the life-worldly, economic and theoretical conditions of modern societies. In a certain sense, the concept functions as a hinge between the analysis of capitalism and the theory of rationality and is used in a social theoretical and rationality-critical way: The critique of the capitalist or modern society and the critique of philosophy, that is, of a certain form of reason, are closely linked. Marx's analyses of commodity fetishism, generalized with recourse to Max Weber's theory of rationalization, are used for a comprehensive diagnosis of the times. Commodities, according to Lukács, permeate all expressions of life of a society. He understands them as a "universal structuring principle" of human society (see Lukács, 1971, p. 85).

If one follows Lukács, commodities structure people's relationships with themselves, with one another, and with society in general. The shape of the commodity imprints the whole of human reality and can, for Lukács, be distinguished into objective and subjective ranges of influence. An alien world of finished things and relationships among them arises for the human being; an objective world with which the human being stands face to face. At the same time, the human being is subjectively alienated from its activities, which now obey the requirements of the fictitious world of things. According to Lukacs, the description of wage labor which Marx developed, especially under the capitalist condition of the division of labour, can be generalized: "The fate of the worker becomes the fate of society as a whole" (*ibid.*, p. 91). All expressions of human life are subject to the process of rationalization and calculability. Lukács finds this exemplified in journalism, modern bureaucracy, and in the law (see, *ibid.*, p. 100).

The broadening of the Marxist analysis presents, however, only a first step in the context of Lukács' attempt at universalization. In a further step, he applies the reification theorem to the sciences and to philosophy.

---

3   See, for this, Brunkhorst and Krockenberger (1998).

Reification should not only be characteristic of the living conditions of human beings but also of a mode of thought that is characteristic for science and a non-dialectical philosophy geared towards the sciences generally. Science and non-dialectical philosophy are seen by Lukács as mirror images of an already inverted world, which only serves to reproduce and solidify its inversion. Just as Marx criticized the real economy and thereby also social conditions and the material appearance which takes hold in them, also pointing to the reproduction of this appearance in theories of political economy, Lukács uses the concept of reification for the critique of real living conditions and for the critical examination of scientific and theoretical developments. From his point of view, an abstract concept of reason and formalistic methodology dominate in law, philosophy, and in the sciences. Lukács classifies them as the rationalist and ideological correlates of the form of the commodity. The organization of labor and of the market extends all the way into the formation of theory. In this context, Lukács is fundamentally guided by the view that all thinking is subject to a social determination of form. In this way, for instance, the substantialist interpretation of our distinctions, the ahistorical understanding of the categories that we use to organize reality, are traced back to the economic processes of reification whose likenesses they are.

From the perspective of his reflections on the universalization of the form of the commodity, Lukács recapitulates parts of the history of modern philosophy. The main points of reference are, in the first place, the development from Kant to Hegel, and additionally and in particular the Neo-Kantianism of the Southwest School of Germany. He is guided by the question of the constitution of modern rationalism. Lukács' considerations demonstrate that he understands, in a particularly powerful way, the question of the categorical pre-formedness of reality and the origin of our forms of thought in the sense of claims regarding the social predeterminedness of thinking. His thesis is that modern rationalism has developed in constant interaction with the development of people's conditions of life and labor and that rationalism has become universal along with the universalization of the commodity. Thus, Lukács is able to reduce classical German philosophy to the "reified structure of consciousness" (*ibid.*, pp. 110 f.). He describes reification on the level of thought, as, among other things, the tendency towards a fixed understanding of conceptual distinctions or the absolutization of dualisms. In this context, one can invoke, for instance, the guiding distinction between subject and object. One can also, however, invoke the empiristic tendency to make the concept of a fact into the basic concept of an investigation of reality, thus assigning philosophy the mere role of a companion to the sciences. Lukács sees a fundamental tendency in that philosophy „acknowledges as given and necessary the results and achievements of the special sciences and assigns to philosophy the task of exhibiting and justifying the grounds for regarding as valid the concepts so constructed. Thus, philosophy stands in the same relation to the special sciences as they do with respect to empirical reality. The formalistic conceptualisation of the special sciences become an immutably given substratum for philosophy and this signals the final and despairing renunciation of every attempt to cast light on the reification that lies at the root of this formalism" (*ibid.*, p.110).

The individual sciences and a philosophy exclusively oriented towards their methods are therefore an object of critique for Lukács because the description of facts typically abstracts from their embeddedness in a historical context. Lukács interprets such a view of facts in analogy with economic reification and asserts that it is necessary to „detach the phenomena from the form in which they are immediately given and discover the intervening links which connect them to their core, their essence" (*ibid.*, p. 8). Only then, when one sees "the isolated facts of social life as aspects of the historical process and integrates them in a totality" does knowledge of reality become possible (*ibid.*). Achieving this, in Lukács view, is reserved for dialectical philosophy.

A number of recent reconstructions of Marx's conception and Lukács' reflections have since become available, which serve to provide detailed explanations of their contents.[4] My aim is not to validate the viability and consistency of the positions in order to accept or reject them. It is merely to recall, in broad strokes, the basic idea behind conceptions of reification inspired by Marx. In the following section I would like to ask whether, in an analogical sense, a reification theorem might be located in other theoretical contexts. To this end, I touch upon various ideas from Wittgenstein, which can be understood as a language-critical variant of the analysis of reification.[5] I also discuss the matter of how the relationship between Wittgenstein's analyses and Marx-inspired reification theories can be specified.

---

4   For Lukács see, Dannemann (1987). For the discussion of Lukács in the context
      of recent developments in critical theory, see, Fuchs (2016). Hartle (2017) and
      Verkerk (2017) make very different attempts towards its revitalization. See, also
      the contributions in the volume Thompson (2011), in particular the introduction.
5   Andrews (2002) provides a revealing analysis in which Marx's reflections in the
      chapter on commodity fetishism are brought into contact with Wittgenstein.

4. *Language and Reification*

Despite a considerable amount of literature which concerns itself with the relationship between Marx and Wittgenstein and discusses both philosophical and biographical questions, the approaches of authors such as Marx and Lukács on the one hand and Wittgenstein on the other seem to lie so far apart that they can hardly be brought to bear on one another.[6] Nevertheless, Wittgenstein's reflections can be understood in the sense of a language-critical reification theory. In Wittgenstein's philosophy, language has a function comparable to that of labor in Marx. Like work, language is a fundamental form of human practice; it is constitutive for the human experience of the world. Wittgenstein's criticism of theories in the philosophy of language which do not take up its practical function and, for instance, disregard the use of language as a source of meaning, exhibits features characteristic of critiques of reification. Marx's reflections are to be understood in the sense of a critique of the development of economic theory, but also in the sense of a critique of real living conditions. The matter is similar with Wittgenstein. The critical meaning of his analyses is not only to be seen in the rejection of certain misconceptions within the philosophy of language regarding the functioning of language, for instance, the name-object theory of meaning, but also consists in liberating us of false theoretical conceptions concerning language, which permeate our real living conditions. His critique of language should not only be recommended as therapy for philosophers, but also concerns the everyday use of language.

It is nonetheless true that Wittgenstein's explicit remarks on the language-critical dimension are primarily directed against the philosophical misuse of language. It is also characteristic of Wittgenstein's understanding of philosophy that he does not see it as a mere theoretical endeavor, but rather regards it as an activity that is always related to the life and the coexistence of human beings. It focuses on the analysis of mechanisms of linguistic hypostatization and reification, which not only play a role in philosophy, but also in human life. His analyses serve, on the one hand, to correct certain ideas in language philosophy, e.g. those advocated in the context of the Vienna Circle. On the other hand, his philosophy concerns the liberation from reified understandings of human life, namely those that are suggested by a mistaken understanding of language. Wittgenstein's

---

6   I refer only to a few texts: Pitkin (1972), Rossi-Landi (1972), Kitching (1988), Kitching & Pleasants (2002), Gakis (2015).

philosophy is therefore critical on the one hand in the sense of critique of philosophy, but on the other as a critique aimed directly at human life. Of course, Wittgenstein's philosophy is a form of language critique that abstracts from historical and social relations in the narrower sense.

According to Wittgenstein, philosophy is primarily about describing the way in which our language works. Misunderstandings, which are determined by the use of language and repeatedly lead to philosophical irritations can be illuminated. Missing or problematic language usage can be recognized and rejected as such. The language-critical dimension of his philosophy is what leads him to the formulation that the philosopher treats questions like diseases. The aim of philosophy is to do away with the sorcery of language, which is seen as the main cause of philosophical, but also of 'everyday' diseases (see, Wittgenstein, 1953, § 255).

Language can 'enchant' in different ways: Established and often unquestioned distinctions, such as that between inner and outer for the characterization of the difference between the mental and the physical can give direction to thought and lead it astray; the thoughtless use of jargon can suggest 'depth' and 'difficulty' despite actual simplicity. A philosophy understood as a critique of language should stem diseases caused by a careless use of language. In this sense, Wittgenstein's philosophy can be viewed as a therapy which aims towards a liberation from constraints on thought and linguistic habits. It achieves this by absolving us of seemingly legitimate questions and distinctions repeatedly forced on us by the philosophical tradition, by way of established theories, but also through the parlance of our scientific and cultural practices.

In the *Philosophical Investigations* all forms philosophical problems are repeatedly traced back to a misunderstood, if not erroneous, use of language. Wittgenstein sees it as a basic evil of philosophical theorizing that words are detached from their usual and everyday use-contexts and embedded in special philosophical and theoretical ones in which they are no longer dealt with in a meaningful way, so that questions arise that irritatingly cannot be answered. These sorts of contexts result when we ask about the essence of something, for instance, the "*essence* of language, of propositions, of thought" (Wittgenstein, 1953, § 92). If one poses these questions, according to Wittgenstein, it can make things appear "as if there were something like a final analysis of our forms of language [...] as if there were something hidden in them that had to be brought to light" (Wittgenstein, 1953, § 91). A therapeutic philosophizing seeks to counter this appearance. The secret or myth of final linguistic forms, which supposedly contain hidden and philosophically informative treasures, is revealed by tracing words back from their philosophical to their everyday use. The procedure aims to clarify and resolve philosophical problems through a linguistic demystification.

> When philosophers use a word – "knowledge", "being", "object", "I", "proposition", "name" – and try to grasp the *essence* of the thing, one must always ask oneself: is the word ever actually used in this way in the language-game which is its original home? – What *we* do is to bring words back from their metaphysical to their everyday usage. (Wittgenstein, 1953, p. 116)

Wittgenstein's reflections sometimes sound as if a mere consideration of the everyday use of words would lead to the resolution of philosophical problems or as if an everyday use is *per se* clearer than philosophical or scientific usages. There are grounds to dispute whether the everyday use of words is the measure of all things. Measured against philosophical standards, the everyday usage of language is often simply unclear and, in most cases, not unambiguous. In addition, everyday uses do not remain unaffected by the perspectives, attitudes, and images that are suggested to us by metaphysical usages. Rather, understandings of the self and of the world seep into everyday language. Accordingly, the language-critical therapy should not only be recommended as a healing measure for the illnesses of professional philosophers but also to clarify the assumptions and implications of everyday speech. One can think, for instance, of the prevalence of the previously mentioned distinction between 'inner' and 'outer' in the context of an attempt to say something about the relationship between mind and body. The distinction is not only widespread in philosophical theories about the mind-body problem but is also an integral part of many everyday self-understandings. It is no less misleading in the latter than in the former.[7]

Quite independently of exegetical questions related to Wittgenstein, I would understand the instruments of language critique from a philosophical perspective such that they do not only aim to correct philosophical and metaphysical usages of linguistic expressions, but rather also aim to expose misguided images and errors that have established themselves in the everyday use of language. Making recourse to everyday uses of 'endangered' words such as 'knowledge', 'sentence', or 'name' does not, therefore, represent a solution to the problems associated with

---

7   The extent to which this "inner/outer" image has spread within and outside of philosophy is accentuated by the reflections of Hubert Dreyfus and Taylor presented in: Dreyfus & Taylor (2015).

metaphysical uses. Rather, the compilation of the use of expressions in everyday language ought to be regarded as a *corrective*. It is a question of retrieving aspects of the meaning of expressions that are embedded in everyday ways of speaking and inferring, in order to gain an overview of the use of these expressions with the goal of bringing order to philosophical questions and erecting a context for them so that they can be released from a self-referential philosophical milieu.

According to Wittgenstein, the task of a philosophy understood as therapy consists in a *grammatical* analysis. His use of the term 'grammar', however, takes some getting used to and is idiosyncratic, going well beyond its usual use, according to which the word 'grammar' denotes the totality of syntactic and morphological rules by means of which the expressions and the parts of expressions of language and can be shaped and brought together. Wittgenstein's use of the concept 'grammar' is nonetheless related to an analysis of the rules and regularities that guide the use of linguistic expressions. These include, however, a semantic dimension in the broadest sense, insofar as the grammar concept becomes a successor, in a certain sense, to talk of the logic of a language.[8] Statements concerning the grammar of language in Wittgenstein's sense are to be strictly distinguished from empirical propositions. They do not elucidate the world, but rather concern the assumptions and conditions for making sense in our thinking, speaking, and acting. The examination of grammatical rules refers to the different combinatorial possibilities of words and sentences and of sentences into larger linguistic units, from which the meaning of expressions ultimately arises. In the context of a grammatical analysis of expressions, it is always a question of exposing the inferential relationships in which the expressions in question stand or may stand and of making clear what one is committed to by the use of words and expressions as well as what they imply.

Philosophy does not necessarily retire following therapeutic philosophizing and the method of grammatical analysis. Instead, its 'workplace' changes. The philosophical theorist who works according to the model of the sciences is replaced by the philosophical grammarian, who observes the use of language in order to make sense of philosophical problems and track down the mistakes that language compels us to make while philosophizing. More specifically, the grammarian examines different mechanisms from which errors in our understanding of language

---

8   A brief overview of Wittgenstein's concept of grammar is given by Glock (2000, pp. 154-159) and Schulte (1989, pp.112-118). On the role of the concept of a philosophical grammar in the development of Wittgenstein's thinking, see Gebauer (2009, pp. 107ff).

can result: the projection of linguistic structures into the world, surface-level grammatical analogies between words, that can, for instance, tempt us into interpreting sensation-words as if they denote things, prejudices that can result from ingrained linguistic habits, images and metaphors that have settled into the language and can no longer be recognized as such, and much more. All of these mechanisms can become the subject of language-critical reflection and in many cases, it can also be proven that a misunderstanding of language can go hand in hand with flawed practices, and even, in some cases, lead to them.

When Wittgenstein glosses philosophy as therapy, he also recognizes it as having an *emancipatory* function. Its task consists in a *liberation* of people from incorrect understandings of themselves and of their language. These therapeutic acts can be understood as paradigms for emancipatory practices, especially in the light of the kind of treatments developed by psychoanalysis. The early Habermas, for instance, sets forth a number of relevant considerations in this context.[9] The emancipatory aspect of the therapeutic treatment remains initially limited to single individuals. Does - I now want to ask - the therapeutic dimension of philosophy in Wittgenstein's sense have a socio-critical purview or a socio-critical potential (even if only in the broadest sense)?

Isn't language criticism a form of philosophical therapy that need only be recommended to the philosopher who fishes in the muddy waters of linguistic hypostasis and is thus led astray? Rather than venturing a hasty and positive answer to this question, it is worth accentuating the fact that language shapes the understanding and consummation of everyday life to a much greater extent than it may appear to do at first glance. The range of distortions and deformations that result from an incorrect understanding of our language is vast. The therapeutic function of language criticism does not, therefore, only affect philosophers. Everyday, and, it should be added, collective systems of belief, are at the mercy of the power of language.

It is only initially surprising that a form of language criticism that is ultimately similar to that of Wittgenstein can already be found in Marx, where it stands in immediate connection to socio-critical reflections.[10] As Marx claims by way of his alienation theorem and with his diagnosis of commodity fetishism, linguistic hypostatizations are to be seen as the result of the real independence of social relations. Marx writes: "All relations

---

9   See, for this, the instructive work of Celikates (2009, pp 195-216).
10   Recent works that read Marx from the point of view of the philosophy of language are relatively rare. See, for instance, Lecercle (2006). A classic work on the subject was published in Russian as early as 1929: Vološinov (1986).

can be expressed in language only in the form of concepts. That these general ideas and concepts are looked upon as mysterious forces is the necessary result of the fact that the real relations, of which they are the expression, have acquired independent existence. Besides this meaning in everyday consciousness, these general ideas are further elaborated and given a special significance by politicians and lawyers, who, as a result of the division of labour, are dependent on the cult of these concepts, and who see in them, and not in the relations of production, the true basis of all real property relations" (Marx & Engels, 1976a, p. 365).

Like Wittgenstein, Marx recommends that those who have succumbed to the "cult of concepts" return the terms to their everyday usage: "The philosophers have only to dissolve their language into the ordinary language, from which it is abstracted, in order to recognize it as the distorted language of the actual world and to realize that neither thoughts nor language in themselves form a realm of their own, that they are only manifestations of actual life" (Marx & Engels 1976a, p. 447). With these remarks, Marx applies his basic conception, initially and paradigmatically developed through the analysis of the commodity, to language. Just as goods do not lead a life of their own in their own realm but are rather products of human practices from which they can only be detached from a reified perspective, language is to be found in the real world and cannot be separated from the everyday practice and usage of its speakers.

Apart from parallels in the critique of language, Marxist ideology critique and social critique in general can also be understood in the sense of a therapeutic measure. Marx's critique of political economy diagnoses societal illnesses that can be cured with the means of philosophy and through enlightenment. The correspondences between institutional constraints at the societal level and neurotic behavior on the individual level are striking. In both cases, rigid behavioral patterns that have been withdrawn from critique are reproduced, causing suffering and giving off the appearance of permanence.

According to Wittgenstein, philosophy is an instrument for resolving difficulties; for him it is not merely a question of solving theoretical riddles, but he rather understands philosophy as a practical labor towards the liberation from misunderstanding occasioned by language. As therapy, philosophy is itself a practice. It is essential to therapeutic practice that it focus on (the reinstatement of) the autonomy of persons. It is a practice with an inherent emancipatory sense, one that aims at enlightenment. The therapeutic measures of philosophy are directed at the liberation of people from their creations. The entanglement of people in the web of language cannot, of course, be resolved; what can be resolved are the deformations that can result from this entanglement. "What is your aim in philosophy? – To shew the fly the way out of the fly-bottle" (Wittgenstein, 1953, § 309). This picture successfully expresses the emancipatory claim of Wittgenstein's philosophy. The fly in the glass is not only a philosopher who misunderstands language, but also stands for all those who are caught in the darkness of linguistic hypostasis. The way out of the glass follows from a liberation from the mistaken self- and world-understandings suggested to us by a mistaken interpretation of language. But can this form of language critique be understood in a socio- or ideology-critical sense at all if one ignores the possibility of relating it to Marx's analyses of alienation and of commodities? In closing, I would like to discuss only one relevant example.

Many of our ways of speaking come with certain attitudes and modes of behavior, such as the idea that certain things correspond to the words as their meanings. What is time? Wittgenstein already detects a tendency towards reification in this question (see Wittgenstein, 1972, p. 26). The noun 'time' suggests the presence of a thing that corresponds to the word. When formulated in this way, time appears as an entity independent of human activity. The formulation of a question like, "What is time?" implies a certain way of behaving towards time. The idea of time as a thing is connected to its quantification. Of course, not every type of quantification of time is associated with a deformation of contexts of human life. In many contexts, however, there are distortions that only become possible through a quantification of time. Time can be saved and stolen. It is no coincidence that Wittgenstein is not the only one to concern himself with the reification of time from the perspective of language-critique. The reification of time, with its deforming consequences, was also discussed by Marx, and, in a broader sense, by critical theory.[11] This is once again an indication that language analysis and critical social theory can lead to similar results when analyzing phenomena. Working time is time petrified into a quantitatively measurable thing, especially where it serves to measure the value of work in the sense of a specific and purposeful action. However, the quantification of time is not limited to working time but penetrates all areas of human life, shaping the biographies of individuals.

---

11   See, Marx (1976b, p.127) for the analysis of the quantification of time as working time; Rosa (2010) provides a more recent contribution to the critique of quantified understandings of time.

Time, which is one-sidedly misunderstood as a thing and subjected to the categories of availability and manageability, leads to different forms of a reified context of life. Life is brought into a dependency on an economically and linguistically reified, quantified time. It is reduced to a time factor, stripping it of any qualitative, experiential referent. With regards to reification theory, both a language-critical analysis and a theory like Marx's criticize the guiding misunderstandings and reconstruct their origins. Wittgenstein's language-critical analyses do not directly involve the elements indicated, but they can nonetheless be philosophically related to problems of social theory.

Translated from German
by Ian Polakiewicz

References

Andrews, D. (2002). Commodity Fetishism as a Form of Life. Language and Value in Wittgenstein and Marx. In G. Kitching & N. Pleasants (Eds.) *Marx and Wittgenstein. Knowledge, Morality, and Politics*. London and New York: Routledge, pp. 78-94.

Brunkhorst, H. & Krockenberger, P. (1998). Paradigm-core and Theory-dynamics in Critical Social Theory: People and Programs. In *Philosophy and Social Criticism*, 24 (6), pp. 67–110.

Celikates, R. (2009). *Kritik als soziale Praxis. Gesellschaftliche Selbstverständigung und kritische Theorie*. Frankfurt am Main: Campus Verlag.

Dannemann, R. (1987). *Das Prinzip Verdinglichung. Studie zur Philosophie Georg Lukács'*. Frankfurt am Main: Sendler.

Demmerling, C. (1994). *Sprache und Verdinglichung. Wittgenstein, Adorno und das Projekt einer kritischen Theorie*. Frankfurt am Main: Suhrkamp.

Demmerling, C. (2014). Philosophie as Therapie. Die Auflösung philosophischer Dualismen. In C. Barth & D. Lauer (Eds.) *Die Philosophie John McDowells. Ein Handbuch*. Münster: Mentis, pp.19-36.

Demmerling, C. (2018). More than Words: from language to Society. Wittgenstein, Marx, and Critical Theory. In D. Kubok (Ed.), *Thinking Critically: What Does It Mean?* Berlin/Boston: De Gruyter, pp. 191-212.

Dreyfus, H. & Taylor, C. (2015). *Retrieving Realism.* Cambridge/Mass.: Harvard University Press.

Fuchs, C. (2016). *Critical Theory of Communication. New readings of Lukács, Adorno, Marcuse, Honneth and Habermas in the Age of the Internet.* London: University of Westminster Press.

Gandesha, S. & Hartle, J. F. (Eds.) (2017). *The Spell of Capital: Reification and Spectacle.* Amsterdam: Amsterdam University Press.

Gakis, D. (2015). Wittgenstein, Marx, and Marxism: Some Historical Connections. In *Humanities 4*, 924–937 (doi:10.3390/h4040924).

Gebauer, G. (2009). *Wittgensteins anthropologisches Denken.* München: Verlag C.H. Beck.

Glock, H. J. (2000). *Wittgenstein-Lexikon.* Darmstadt: Wissenschaftliche Buchgesellschaft.

Hartle, J. F. (2017). Reification as Structural Depoliticization: The Political Ontology of Lukács and Debord. In Gandesha D. & Hartle J. F. (Eds.), *The Spell of Capital: Reification and Spectacle.* Amsterdam: Amsterdam University Press, pp. 21-36.

Honneth, A. (2005). *Verdinglichung. Eine anerkennungstheoretische Studie.* Frankfurt am Main: Suhrkamp.

Kitching, G. & Pleasants, N. (Eds.) (2002). *Marx and Wittgenstein. Knowledge, Morality, and Politics.* London and New York: Routledge.

Kitching, G. (2015). *Karl Marx and the Philosophy of Praxis.* London and New York: Routledge.

Lecercle, J.-J. (2006). *A Marxist Philosophy of Language.* Leiden: Brill.

Lukács, G. (1971). *History and Class Consciousness. Studies in Marxist Dialectics,* trans. R. Livingstone. Cambridge/Mass: MIT Press.

Marx, K. & Engels, F. (1976a). The German Ideology. In K. Marx & F. Engels, *Collected Works* (Vol. 5), trans. C. Dutt, W. Lough and C. P. Magill. London: Lawrence & Wishart.

Marx, K. (1976b). The Poverty of Philosophy. In K. Marx & F. Engels, *Collected Works* (Vol 6). London: Lawrence & Wishart.

Marx, K. & Engels, F. (2010). Economic and Philosophic Manuscripts of 1844. In K. Marx & F. Engels, *Collected Works* (Vol. 3), trans. M. Mulligan and D. J. Struik. London: Lawrence & Wishart.

Marx, K. & Engels, F. (2010a). Capital. Volume I. In K. Marx & F. Engels, *Collected Works* (Vol. 35), transl. S. Moore and E. Aveling. London: Lawrence & Wishart.

Marx, K. & Engels, F. (2010b). Capital. Volume III. In K: Marx & F. Engels, *Collected Works* (Vol. 37), trans. E. Untermann. London: Lawrence & Wishart.

Marx, K. & Engels, F. (1964). *Werke*. Band 25: Das Kapital III. Berlin: Dietz Verlag.

Pitkin, H. F. (1972). *Wittgenstein and Justice. On the Significance of Ludwig Wittgenstein for Social and Political Thought*. Berkeley: University of California Press.

Quadflieg, D. (2019). V*om Geist der Sache. Kritik der Verdinglichung*. Frankfurt/New York: Campus Verlag.

Rosa, H. (2010). *Alienation and Acceleration. Towards a Critical Theory of Late-Modern Temporality*. Aarhus: NSU Press.

Rossi-Landi, F. (1972). *Sprache als Arbeit und als Markt*. München: Carl Hanser Verlag.

Rubinstein, D. (1981). *Marx and Wittgenstein. Social Praxis and Social Explanation*. London and Boston: Routledge and Kegan Paul.

Schulte, J. (1989). *Wittgenstein. Eine Einführung*. Stuttgart: Reclam.

Thompson, M. J. (2011). *Georg Lukács Reconsidered. Critical Essays in Politics, Philosophy and Aesthetics*. London and New York: Continuum.

Verkerk, W. (2017). Reification, Sexual Objectivication, and Feminist Activism. In S. Gandesha and J. F. Hartle (Eds.), *The Spell of Capital: Reification and Spectacle*. Amsterdam: Amsterdam University Press, pp. 149-161.

Vološinov, V. N. (1986*). Marxism and the Philosophy of language*. Cambridge/Mass.: Harvard University Press.

Wittgenstein, L. (1922). *Tractatus Logico-Philosophicus*, trans. C. K. Ogden and F. Ramsey. London, Kegan Paul, London: Harcourt.

Wittgenstein, L. (1953). *Philosophische Untersuchungen/Philosophical Investigations*, trans. G. E. M. Anscombe. Oxford: Blackwell.

Wittgenstein, L. (1972). *The Blue and Brown Books*. Oxford: Blackwell.

4.
LANGUAGE BETWEEN CRITICAL THEORY
AND SOCIAL SCIENCES

LOTAR RASIŃSKI

BEYOND CRITICAL THEORY
Wittgenstein, Discourse Ethics and Emancipatory Practice[1]

1. *Introduction*

The aim of this paper is to explore the possibilities of critical reflection on politics and democracy alternative to the currently dominant model of critical theory. While many of contemporary critical theory postulates, especially in the variety represented by Jürgen Habermas, seem to be unquestionable – e.g. the attempt to seek balance between the republican and liberal models of politics, or to search for a democratic *modus operandi* in the pragmatics of language – I argue that this approach excessively invests in "the search for foundations," i.e. it devotes too much attention to establishing theoretical grounds which would make the theory into a universal tool for assessing societies, while ignoring existing and new-emerged social and political practices and developments. This approach, rooted in Kantian project of critical reflection, builds on the ideas of unity of rationality and of universal status of claims of reason, which are becoming more and more questionable in contemporary political reflection, where the problems of cultural and political diversity and the lack of trust to the established democratic institutions constitute the most demanding challenges (Mouffe, 2013; Mouffe, 2019; Wilson and Swyngedouw (eds.), 2014; Walzer, 2006; Rosanvallon, 2008). The principles of rationalism and universalism can be seen as exclusive when transferred onto the socio-political domain, since they entail an automatic marginalisation of all "non-rational" voices and stances which defy inscription in the "rational agreement," formed in "ideal speech situation" or "practical discourse." Critical theory and the politics based on these concepts fails to explain, I argue, the anti-elitist, populist and authoritarian tendencies based on

1   The work on this article was supported by National Science Centre, Poland, under research project "Wittgenstein and Democratic Politics," no. UMO-2018/30/M/HS1/00781.

emotions and distrust to political elites present in the social moods of many European countries today.

In the first part of the paper I briefly describe the very idea of Habermas' "discourse ethics" and then use Wittgenstein's perspective to critically discuss four arguments which are in my opinion crucial for Habermas' understanding of deliberative politics: firstly, Habermas's distinction between "everyday communicative practice" and "practical discourse;" secondly, his proclamation of the universal validity of norms developed in discourse as an expression of common rationality; thirdly, his recognition as rational only these statements which are rationally justified; and, fourthly, Habermas's assumption that the principles of discourse ethics which regulate the democratic deliberation processes are "purely formal."

In the second part of the paper, I demonstrate an idea of *emancipatory practice* as an alternative to understanding of critique as proposed by critical theory of Jürgen Habermas. The idea ensues from an apparently peculiar juxtaposition of Marx's and Wittgenstein's critical projects. I believe that the two philosophies are fundamentally interrelated in two ways. First of all they both insist that it is practice that determines the shape of our thought. Secondly, they both criticize all manifestations of metaphysical thinking in philosophy. I argue that both Marx's and Wittgenstein's philosophies are unique practice-oriented critical enterprises, which, when understood in their mutual supplementation, could open up possibilities of thinking about social criticism in ways alternative to the traditional critical theory.[2]

Marx defines critique as "the reform of consciousness" and identifies emancipation as a unique practical purpose of and a reason for criticism. I will provide an example of a Wittgenstein-inspired reading of Marx by referring to the concepts of alienation and ideology. The "Wittgenstein-filtered" alienation would basically reside in misrecognition, that is, in human failure to realize that alienness of objects and people generated by human labour is an illusion. Similarly, we can think of ideology critique not as a theory of cognition of real class interests and relations of production, but rather as a way of understanding reality recognizing multiplicity of aspects and dissolving "aspect blindness." Wittgenstein's postulate of „returning to ordinary language" helps us also free Marx's thinking on emancipation from the burden of what we could call the "philosophy of the Subject," to use Seyla Benhabib formulation (Benhabib, 1984, p. 285). However, I

---

2   There is already significant scholarship on the connections between Marx and
     Wittgenstein, (see esp. Kitching, Pleasants, 2002; Rossi-Landi, 1992; Rossi-
     Landi, 1983; Rubinstein, 1981; Sen, 2003, pp. 1240-1255).

argue, it could also be valuable to read Wittgenstein through Marx, which would entail perceiving Wittgenstein's therapy in emancipatory terms. In this sense, „the return to ordinary language" propounded by Wittgenstein carries the seeds of liberation. "Wittgensteinian emancipation" would involve language ceasing to be an alien being that hinders our self-expression.

The mutually complemented reading of Marx and Wittgenstein helps us recognize problems inherent in Marx's idea of emancipation as a reason and as a purpose for criticism and identify promising political uses of Wittgenstein's concepts. In conclusion, I demonstrate how Wittgenstein's concepts of therapy and "perspicuous presentation" and Marx's idea of "political emancipation" can be useful in understanding Foucault's project of genealogy and his idea of "expanding the limits of freedom".

2. The context – "discourse ethics" and everyday language

Of course, to state that Habermas's discourse ethics is exclusive or elitist may sound rather contentious. Jürgen Habermas is the leading architect of contemporary democratic theory with democracy posited as the cornerstone of a just and impartial social order. However, I am not so much distrustful about the very idea of deliberative politics or procedural democracy, as rather apprehensive of the political consequences of the abstract and metaphysical assumptions of the Habermasian project which allow to connect it with exclusivist tendencies of contemporary liberal democracies.

Habermas's concept of discourse ethics derives directly from the theory of communicative action with a critique of Weber's theory of action lying at the heart of it. Originating in the intentionalist theory of consciousness, Weber's framework, according to Habermas, fails to capture any activity beyond that of "the solitary acting subject" (Habermas, 1984, p. 279). Habermas thus proposes an alternative to Weber's typology of action,[3] supplementing the rational goal-oriented action (such as instrumental and strategic action) with the equally important understanding-oriented action, i.e. communicative action. In Habermas's view, communicative actions cannot be reduced to the instrumental or strategic dimensions, because their

---

3   The classical ("official," as Habermas puts it) Weberian typology distinguishes the following categories of action: instrumentally-rational, value-rational, affectual and traditional, (see Weber 1978, pp. 24-25). Cfr. Habermas, (1984, p. 281).

participants co-ordinate action plans not on the basis of egocentric pursuit of calculated success but through acts in which understanding is established in the "negotiation of common definitions of situations" (Habermas, 1984, p. xxiv). Moreover communicative action is in fact constitutive of strategic and instrumental action. Habermas infers such conclusions from linguistic analyses, and in particular from Austin's speech act theory, which distinguishes between illocutionary and perlocutionary acts. He assumes that the illocutionary effect is a precondition of the perlocutionary effect, and hence, that for an statement to be included in the scope of goal-oriented actions, it must first become a communicative action (see *ibid.*, p. 483).

Communicative action, according to Habermas, must presume that language is "a medium of a kind of reaching understanding" (*ibid.*, p. 99) engaged in which its participants raise mutual validity claims. A claim of validity can be raised, usually implicitly, by a speaker in relation to at least one listener. Due to triadic reference to the world, Habermas enumerates three types of validity claims: to the truth of the statement (i.e., that it adequately represents some beings or states of affairs), to the rightness of the statement (i.e., that it obeys the norms and rules of discourse valid in a given community), and to the sincerity of the statements (i.e., that the actual intentions are identical with the expressed ones) (see *ibid.*, pp. 99-100; cfr. *ibid.*, p. 308).

Reaching understanding (consensus) and the claims of validity intrinsic to it[4] provide a ground, as Habermas postulates, for critical reflection which allows us to determine whether our actions are free and rational. To put it simply, Habermas believes that if a human conversation is to make any sense, people *must* seek to understand each other, presume that they tell the truth and assume that their behavior complies with the existing norms. "Reaching understanding is the inherent *telos* of human speech" (Habermas, 1984, p. 287). Each conversation presumes that there are at least two conscious and rational subjects who, in good faith, strive to communicate with each other in order to undertake this or that action together. The understanding arrived at in communication cannot be *imposed* by either of the parties involved, nor can it ensue from instrumental or strategic action (see *ibid.*, p. 475).

Habermas, however, allows moments in which the "critical deliberation," which is a condition of understanding, does not come to pass. In *A Reply to my Critics*, he recognizes what he calls "the communicative practice

---

4   Sometimes Habermas lists also a fourth claim – one of comprehensibility, (cfr. Habermas, 1974, p. 18).

of everyday life … immersed in a sea of cultural taken-for-grantedness" (Habermas, 1982, pp. 272-273). It is, as he puts it, "lifeworld background of actual processes of reaching understanding" (*ibid.*). These everyday communicative practices do not require critical reflection and are based on certainties, agreements and customs. However, when this "pre-reflexive" knowledge comes to be transformed into the "semantic content of the statement," entering thereby the scope of "discourse," the certainties and sooths of this common knowledge are subjected to critical judgment. Hence whether our everyday practices are rational or not depends on whether we can supply a justification for them, i.e., state that they fulfill the three validity claims. As Habermas sees it, the rationality of communication depends on our capability to justify our statements by means of rational argumentation. This entails questioning the "taken-for-grantedness" of our everyday practices at the same time.

The central tenet of the Habermasian discourse ethics is that it is not the force of custom, but rather the "unforced force of the better argument" that counts in discourse (Habermas, 1998, p. 306). Therefore, "a communicatively achieved agreement must be based in the end on reasons" (Habermas, 1984, p. 17). We could state that the argumentation-based practice of rational critique of validity claims is in itself "unconditional," because "justifications are themselves justified" (Tully, 2008, pp. 46-47; cfr. Habermas, 1995, pp. 19-20) by the structure of the communicative act.[5] What is more, as Habermas states, "the validity claims that we raise in conversation – that is when we say something with conviction – transcend this specific conversational context, pointing to something beyond the spatio-temporal ambit of the occasion" (Habermas, 1995, p. 19). The justifications that Habermas speaks about are transcendent and universal and, hence, such factors as the social context or the historical situation cannot undermine them. Habermas elaborates on this disputable statement in his theory of "discourse ethics."

Positing a distinction between our "everyday practices" and "critical reflection," Habermas assumes that the point of critical reflection is to question our common use of words and to satisfy the validity claims raised in understanding-oriented speech acts. Only when rationally grounded, can our words become part of understanding which founds a criticism of our practices. It seems thus that in everyday contexts, we deal with two dimensions or levels of language, or to put it differently – with language and meta-language. The major problem to be addressed here is our entry into

---

5   "Discourse is condition of the unconditioned" (Habermas, 1974, p. 19).

"discourse", i.e., the moment when everyday speech practice transforms into critical reflection that necessitates a game of justifications. For Habermas discourse is something more "serious" than ordinary language.[6] As Habermas puts it: "Discourses are performances in which we seek to ground our cognitive utterances" (Habermas, 1974, p. 18). In discourse, the participants do not trade information, do not perform or direct any actions and do not convey any experiences; instead, "they search for arguments or offer justifications"(*ibid.*). Only such an "unreal" or "counterfactual" communication form guarantees a consensus that could possibly be deemed "rational." Habermas called such a counterfactual communication situation "ideal situation of discourse" (*ibid.*, p. 19) or "ideal speech situation" (Habermas, 2001, pp. 97-98). The wording of the phrases was purposefully chosen because the very act of entering into discourse indispensably requires a certain idealization. For our everyday language to become discourse, the following conditions (or rules) must be met:

> Every subject with the competence to speak and act is allowed to take part in a discourse.
> Everyone is allowed to question any assertion whatever.
> Anyone is allowed to introduce any assertion whatever into the discourse.
> Everyone is allowed to express his attitudes, desires and needs.
> No speaker may be prevented, by internal or external coercion, from exercising his right as laid down. (Habermas, 1999, p. 89)

In discourse, nobody is excluded from the discussion, no voices are preferred over other ones, and nobody can be manipulated or pressured into endorsing this or that argument. The only limits demarcated in discourse are those of "the force of the better argument," while the procedure of argumentation, as Habermas puts it, is "self-correcting," which means that participants in a conversation are free to change its rules throughout in order to facilitate understanding.

The so-called discourse ethics principle (D) is according to Habermas more general than other principles that regulate moral or legal norms. The latter actually are derived from the principle of discourse ethics (see Habermas, 1998, ch. 3). As early as in *Theorie und Praxis*, Habermas argued that the rules of discourse characteristic of communicative rationality are central to the democratic process. In *Between Facts and Norms*, he states that procedural democracy involves "institutionalization of the

---

6   It is a moment when Habermas' concept of discourse becomes close to Foucault's, (see Dreyfus and Rabinow, 1983, p. 58).

corresponding procedures and conditions of communication" (*ibid.*, p. 298), which is supposed to warrant that the democratic process will render rational outcomes. The rules of discourse that govern communication acts become, thus, a model for the formal functioning of the democratic process and the debate on it in the public sphere.

3. *Discourse ethics and language game*

Now I would like to revisit the Habermasian idea of discourse, scrutinizing it in the framework provided by Wittgenstein's critique of language. Given Wittgenstein's statements about practice of language, I find four points of Habermas's concept disputable: firstly, Habermas's distinction between everyday communicative practice and practical discourse; secondly, Habermas's proclamation of the universal validity of norms developed in discourse as an expression of common rationality; thirdly, acknowledgement as rational that only which is rationally justified; and fourthly, in the light of the previous three points, the assertion that the principles of discourse ethics which regulate the democratic deliberation processes are "purely formal."

As far as the first objection is concerned separation discourse from everyday language seems a disputable gesture, which marks the former as "a different kind of language" in which meanings are established in negotiation and all beliefs are ultimately justified. We could ask whether such "separation" is viable in the first place, and whether words can at all be used beyond the context of their everyday usage. Besides, where does Habermas's framework position all those who, for whatever reason, are incapable of engaging in the elite game of rational argumentation, which is the groundwork of understanding? Is the sophisticated skill of formulating "the better argument" a truly democratic and commonly accessible value?

Defining "everyday communicative practice" in terms of certain pre-reflexive knowledge which must transform into discourse, Habermas means that the fundamental use of language ("original mode", *telos*) is the use oriented to understanding, while all other possibilities of using language (e.g. strategic or instrumental ones) "are parasitic" upon it (Habermas, 1984, p. 288). It would not be too far-fetched, then, to state that everyday language, as "immersed in a sea of cultural taken-for-grantedness" (Habermas, 1982, pp. 272-273), is in a way "parasitic" upon discourse in Habermas's view. However, Wittgenstein teaches us that exactly the opposite is the case. One of the major problems

Wittgenstein tackles in *Philosophical Investigations* is a critique of what he calls "metaphysical use of language." A philosopher's role, Wittgenstein contends, is to "bring words back from their metaphysical to their everyday use" (Wittgenstein, 1986, § 116). And because language is *a practice* ("the *speaking* of language is part of an activity, or of a form of life" (*ibid.*, § 23), i.e. something that serves a particular aim, be it communication, description, or information, all non-practical language uses (e.g., situations in which we want to describe language itself or beings that usually are not objects of language games or forms of life) parasitically exploit language. In such instances, it is "theory" that is parasitic upon "practice," so to say. According to Wittgenstein, metaphysics has no life of its own, and being only a certain illusion, it must derive its reality from our everyday language – it exists only as an appearance of everyday language.

As far as my second objection is concerned, Habermas claims that the agreement developed within discourse not only determines the norms and standards of conduct in a given community, but also attains the status of universality as an expression of general human rationality. A recourse to the (Winch-mediated) dispute which unfolded between Wittgenstein, on the one hand, and Habermas and Karl-Otto Apel, on the other, in the 60s will shed some light on the point. Peter Winch's *The Idea of a Social Science and its Relation to Philosophy* (1958), though rather coldly received by most positivist-minded social scientists, stirred some interest in German philosophers, who appreciated, unlike the rest of the readership, a critical potential of Wittgenstein's thought as interpreted by Winch. They found it attractive primarily because it opened new, and novel, ways of addressing the concept of *Verstehen*. It could contribute a missing sociological dimension to the concept, serving as an effective supplement and a counterweight to then dominant "psychologizing" interpretation of *Verstehen* propounded by Schleiermacher and Dilthey. The controversial point Habermas and Apel refused to accept, however, was Wittgenstein's concept of "language games", which they saw as fraught with relativist ramifications. Apel argued that if language games constituted upon their own rules are multiple and diverse, a "transcendental unity of various game horizons" (Apel, 1980, p. 165) – or simply a "transcendental language game"[7] – must exist if we are to understand these games as separate from each other and based on their own specific respective rules. Similarly, Habermas believed that the closedness of language games must be breached in order to find

---

7   *Ibid.*, p. 247. Wittgenstein explicitly rejects the existence of such beings (cfr. Wittgenstein, 1965, p. 28).

something that binds them all. This common element which is at the same time a transcendental prerequisite of the multiplicity of language games, allows us to ascribe the modern understanding of the world to the "claim of universality" (Habermas, 1984, pp. 44-45).

This discussion demonstrates how Wittgenstein's concept of "a language game" problematizes Habermas's concept of discourse. According to Nyíri, one of the most prominent Wittgenstein scholars, who initiated so-called conservative interpretations of Wittgenstein's philosophy, the Wittgensteinian concept of rule admonishes us that there are no non-social, universal norms of conduct applicable to all cultures and, consequently, to all "language games." In Wittgenstein, speaking of various "language games" is tantamount to speaking of various "forms of life". Participation in this or that language game has thus its existential and social dimensions, that is, not only language is at stake in it. A language game is a "set of social conventions governing our linguistic practices" (Crary, 2000, p. 119). If we agree that thinking is "consciousness developed through language" (Rossi-Landi, 1992, p. 103), then human understanding or reason is thus by no means an inviolable, autonomous bulwark of humanity or a common plane allowing determination of moral norms or provision of universally credible justifications of our statements. Throughout our lifetime, we are bound to meet people whose standards of rationality will diverge from ours. The sense they make of reality often differs so drastically from the sense we make of it that the gap is impossible to bridge and understanding impossible to achieve through rational deliberation.[8] We simply inhabit different worlds, which can by no means be reconciled or combined, and these worlds are largely *incommensurable*. To be able to respond meaningfully to these people's moral, religious or simply everyday practices, we would need a common plane of understanding, be it one universal human rationality manifest, for example, in an ethically, politically or mathematically neutral language, as Habermas and Apel would argue. However, everyday practice teaches us that difficulties with understanding of others' practices is our common experience. To make sense of practices which are culturally/ethically/economically alien to us is a hope, or a delusion perhaps, that Wittgenstein effectively dispels: there is no universal language (like the language of logic that *Tractatus* seemed to espouse), and instead there are many different language games which institute their own rules and their own rationality standards. To convey this situation, Wittgenstein resorts sometimes to the terminology of family resemblance: "Instead of

---

8   See Wittgenstein's example of wood sellers, (cfr. Wittgenstein, 2001, § 149, 150).

producing something common to all that we call language, I am saying that these phenomena have no one thing in common which makes us use the same word for all,– but that they are *related* with one another in many different ways" (Wittgenstein, 1986, § 65).

As far the third objection is concerned – i.e. tying rationality to justification (see Habermas, 1984, pp. 17-18) – the consequence of such assumption is that all those who fail to justify their reasons within free and unconstraint discussion (for example, the people with mental disability) are barred from benefiting from the consensus reached within discourse because, by definition, they are consigned beyond the order of rationality. Similarly, political voices motivated, for example, by passions are excluded from democratic processes because they build on other values than "the force of the better argument". I would like to use here an amusing example provided by James Tully, who emphatically shows how Wittgenstein's considerations on justification undermine Habermas's thesis. Tully offers us to imagine that at an academic conference Jurgen Habermas starts his presentation from introducing himself, upon which occasion somebody from the audience most trivially questions his claim to sincerity and suggests that Habermas is not who he claims to be. Habermas would reply that obviously he is none other than Habermas. At this point, we could wonder what kind of grounding of sincerity (and truth) claim would effectively and satisfactorily settle the issue. Tully enumerates a range of possible absurd justifications – inspecting the birth certificate, credentials issued by an office, a polygraph test, etc. Whichever of them is selected, the problem continues because we could keep inquiring why this particular justification mode is deemed superior to others. The story is, admittedly, ridiculous and pictures an apparently irrational situation. But "that is precisely my point" (Tully, 2008, p. 48), as Tully remarks. It would be irrational to raise such doubts about the sincerity of a conference speaker wearing a "Jürgen Habermas" badge. No one in their right senses would question the truth and sincerity Habermas's statement in such circumstances. On the contrary, the truth and sincerity of such a statement would be taken for granted as natural and indubitable. Consequently, it turns out that in a practical discourse situation – and a scientific conference is a case of discourse *par excellence* – it may be fully *rational* to acknowledge something as obvious without any ultimate justifications.

Whether it is at all possible to explain or justify one's own statements ultimately begs further considerations. The (im)possibility of ultimate justification of a definition (which in Habermas is presented as justification of norms or words used in practical discourse) is classically illustrated in Wittgenstein's remarks about explaining the term "Moses," which he engages in when discussing the concept of the rule. Irrespective of how precise our definition will be, the application of particular words in it will forever raise doubts:

> As though an explanation as it were hung in the air unless supported by another one. Whereas an explanation may indeed rest on another one that has been given, but none stands in need of another – unless *we* require it to prevent a misunderstanding. One may say: an explanation serves to remove or to avert a misunderstanding – one, that is, that would occur but for the explanation; not every one I can imagine. (Wittgenstein, 1986, § 87)

Explicating or justifying one's stance is more of a pragmatic need of a specific moment than a universal demand of conversation. Using a particular word, or following a particular rule that underlies our actions, does not depend in the least on whether we provide some *ultimate rationale* that justifies it. Certainly, we do not always comply with the rules which have been rationally agreed on and endorsed. Wittgenstein repeatedly emphasizes that there are situations in which no motivation or justification for our actions can be provided: "If I have exhausted the justifications I have reached bedrock and my spade is turned. Then I am inclined to say 'This is simply what I do" (*ibid.*, § 217). And elsewhere: "He must go on like that *without a reason*. Not, however, because he cannot yet grasp the reason but because – in *this* system – there is no reason. ('The chain of reasons comes to an end') (Wittgenstein, 1975, § 301). Or: "When I obey a rule, I do not choose. I obey the rule *blindly*" (Wittgenstein, 1986, § 219).

As far as my fourth objection is concerned, in the light of the previous charges, the claim that the principles of discourse ethics which regulate the democratic discussion processes are "purely formal" is hardly convincing. Relying on Wittgenstein's reflection on the "rule following" and "general terms" (*ibid.*, § 85), Mouffe argues that any kind of agreement is a collection of voices based on the common form of life rather than abstract force of reason – it is rather *Enstimmung* than *Einverstand* (Mouffe, 2000, p. 70). Procedures are "complex ensembles of practices" produced by "specific forms of individuality and identity" (*ibid.*, p. 69), and they are not created top-down, but just function as certain "abridgements of practices" (*ibid.*, p. 68). This diverges from deliberation and procedures envisioned by Habermas, for whom procedures are, basically speaking, institutionalized, purely formal rules of free communication which do not impose any constraints on the object and scope of debate. Hence, as entirely impartial rules, they form the basis for the legitimizing of democratic institutions, ensuring that in the democratic deliberation process the discourse rules are transparent and equally reflect the interest of all citizens. However, if we heed Wittgenstein's statements, the procedures themselves will be revealed as carrying a "substantial ethical commitment" (see *ibid.*, p. 69) and expressive of positing priority to some values over other ones. According to Mouffe, the preference in the case of Habermas involves priority of "the right over the good" (*ibid.*, p. 68).

4. *Back to Marx, through Wittgenstein*

Referring to Wittgenstein, I sought to demonstrate those elements of Habermas's conception which explicitly confirm an "overly theorized" character of his critical project. Its liberal vision of elitist consent of rational individuals may not be entirely satisfying now that the primary challenge to democracy does not lie in expanding it onto new corners of the world, but in sustaining it where democratic tradition has apparently been entrenched for years. Undoubtedly, one of the major sources of the current crisis in democratic project is discrepancy between the views of people as the democratic subject and the aims and interests of political representation and institutions. In this context, Habermasian concept of rational agreement does not help bridge the gap between people's ideas and politicians' ideas. Furthermore, such a proposal, implying superiority of rational subjects versed in argumentation and rhetoric over the frequently emotion-driven rest of society, deepens also the gap between theory and practice, a split which has caused a fundamental difficulty in political reflection since Plato. Repeatedly re-cast over centuries, the motif was probably most fully captured by Karl Marx, especially in the context of his critique of ideology. I believe that it would be worthwhile to revisit his concepts in this context, bearing in mind, however, Wittgenstein's critique of "craving for generality" (Wittgenstein, 1965, pp. 17-18).

Reservations concerning the Marxian project in its standard reading are best expressed by Seyla Benhabib:

> I want to argue that among those normative presuppositions of classical Marxism which must be abandoned today is the Philosophy of the Subject. While contemporary Marxism has done much to displace or replace the paradigm of production, less attention has been paid to the implications of this critique of production for the Marxian concept of the subject – again as an empirical and a normative category. (Benhabib, 1984, p. 285)

The "Philosophy of the Subject" presupposes a uniform model of human action, which can be labeled as "production", and frames the creation of history as an outcome of the single subject's – humanity's – action. In this sense, the proletariat as conceived by Marx does not differ essentially from the Hegelian Spirit (*Geist*) (see *ibid.*, p. 296.), which Marx's reliance on the concept of "species-being" (*Gattungswesen*) only attests to. As Benhabib contends, Marx fails to evade Hegel-inspired normative thinking about the subject even in his *Capital*.

What remains in Marx to hold on to if we abandon his idea of the proletariat as a universal subject of emancipation? I believe that the essential Marxian motif which still proves fruitfully pertinent to critical thinking is his concept of criticism as *an emancipatory practice*. In Marx's writings, reflection on criticism appears first of all in his considerations on emancipation and ideology. In the case of the former, criticism as "a practice of becoming conscious of the meanings of one's own actions" (see Marx, 1997, p. 214) is to serve specific political ends and is part of broader processes in which liberation of humankind is effected. In the case of the latter, criticism is an instrument for demystifying reality, a distorted image of which is fabricated by "ideological apparatus" (Althusser, 1994) for the benefit of the ruling class. Of course, both these tasks are interrelated and imply a strictly practical sense of Marx's critical enterprise. Yet, the latter understanding of criticism is, in my view, less convincing than the former because it is informed by a concept of ideology with its metaphysical premise of a "natural state" of society, a vantage point from which one can grasp the genuine picture of social relations (cfr. Owen, 2007, pp. 89-91). For Marx, economy as scientific and objective perspective on society offers such a vantage point and this universalist and foundationalist understanding of critique is closely connected with the Kantian project, which was later carried on by Habermas.

Criticism in its former sense can be traced in Marx's early writings, in which the critical project targets the practice of transforming people's consciousness rather than the search for society's "Archimedean point". Its basic assumption is linking criticism and emancipation, which becomes its rationale and its end at the same time. Of course, the motif of dispelling the delusions, characteristic as it is of the "ideological" understanding of criticism, emerges here as well, but it is the practical goal of emancipation and not the pursuit of theoretical groundings of the critical project that is brought to the foreground. The concept of criticism in Marx's early writings appears as a synonym of "theory" or "philosophy", which both are justified insofar as they are in fact "actualized" or produce genuine effects in the world, becoming superfluous in the realm of speculation. In his letter to Ruge, Marx describes criticism as "a reform of consciousness", elucidating the difference between his critical project and the projects put forward by Young Hegelians and Utopian Socialists:

> In that case we do not confront the world in a doctrinaire way with a new principle: Here is the truth, kneel down before it! We develop new principles for the world out of the world's own principles. [...] The reform of consciousness consists *only* in making the world aware of its own consciousness, in awakening it out of its dreams about itself, in *explaining* to it the meaning of its own actions. (Marx, 1997, p. 214)

"The reform of consciousness" approximates an awakening from a dream, a direct insight into one's own situation and grasping the meaning of one's action. Marx clearly states that his criticism does not entail imposing an arbitrary ideal, some "new principles" for the world to pursue. In his conception, at least at the level of premises, nothing new is to be added to what is already there in practice. The point is to offer the world an elucidation of *its own* actions.

A recourse to Wittgenstein's concept of "perspicuous representation"[9] may help us better grasp the Marxian idea of criticism as "a reform of consciousness". Baker defines perspicuous representation as "the power to condense something complex into a simple and manageable symbol" (Baker, 2004, p. 23), so that a certain image becomes comprehensible to us. According to Hutto (2007), this power requires a certain kind of "ordering invention", which goes beyond a simple depiction. Hence, I understand "representation" in an activist mode as "ordering" or "arranging" of our grammatical rules so that they help us find our way about a given language game. In this sense, representation would be more than just focusing on a detail that has eluded us[10] – it would demand a certain "creative act" from a philosopher, an act that would then serve as a signpost for our actions.

---

9   In German – übersichtliche Darstellung. Wittgenstein derived this concept from Goethe's "ur-plant" as a certain pattern, "a norm for all other objects" which are central to the learning process. Wittgenstein uses this term rather rarely. In *Philosophical Investigations*, he declares that "the concept of perspicuous representation is of fundamental significance to us" (Wittgenstein, 1986, § 122). He gives more attention to it in *Philosophical Remarks* (1998, § 1-3), where he refers to a colour-octahedron as an example of a general representation of the "grammar of colour."

10   As in Wittgenstein's famous duck-rabbit figure often referred to by the proponents of the so-called elucidatory reading (see Hutchinson and Read, 2008, p. 143).

In *Philosophical Investigations*, Wittgenstein describes "perspicuous representation" also as "assembling reminders for a particular purpose" (Wittgenstein, 1986, § 127). Perspicuous representation, as a certain mode of practicing philosophy, does not consist in enforcing a new vision against a vision that captivates our thinking, but first and foremost in *spotting other possibilities* ("identifying relationships") of making sense of one's own situation. It aims to liberate us from captivating notions (Wittgenstein speaks of "a picture [which] held us captive" (*ibid.*, § 115)), which render our situation in terms of necessity, inherence or inevitability, insisting that "things *must/cannot* be thus and so" (Baker, 2004, p. 34). However, the demonstration of there being other possibilities must always refer to "particular cases" (Wittgenstein, 1965, p. 23). Perspicuous representation is not able to offer us a "bird's eye view" of our grammar, that is, to provide us with universal and generally applicable depictions of operations of our language. It is rather accurate "mapping work," in which a map of a certain area is charted allowing us to "find our way" in a particular situation which offers itself as an inevitable or the only possible one. Such maps always pertain to particular cases and yet they have a capacity to liberate us from images that "hold us captive" by opening up a space of freedom, that is, by pointing at possibilities of thinking, acting or governing in different way.

Let us apply now the Wittgensteinian concept of perspicuous representation to Marx's idea of criticism. I am going to use early Marx's notion of alienation as an application of his understanding of critique as reform of consciousness. Alienation is particularly tainted with the fallacy that Seyla Benhabib calls the "philosophy of the subject." According to Ferruccio Rossi-Landi, the Marxian alienation is a kind of "false consciousness," (Rossi-Landi, 1992, p. 103) which is formed when "anything goes wrong at the level of consciousness" (*ibid.*). The disturbance leads to an incorrect perception of reality. Yet, if we heed Wittgenstein's concept of perspicuous representation, an alternative to this state of affairs need not be grasping metaphysical Truth ("true consciousness"), that is, for example, *Gattungswesen* as a universal human subject which determines the shape of history. An alternative may be offered by perceiving a *differently represented* reality, ie. by seeing different arrangements of elements within the perceived picture. Marx's concept of alienation may be understood as a form of perspicuous representation, which, in a simplified way, provides us with another view of the capitalist world and differently organizes relations among its particular visible components. In this way, Marks would talk of *returning to practice* from the metaphysical and ideological heights, without voicing an overriding, supreme, true, *external* perspective (of science of economy or of species being as undistorted pattern of humanity). He would rather advocate perceiving something we fail to perceive even though "it is always before one's eyes." (Wittgenstein, 1986, § 129). In a sense, alienation compels us to adopt *a position external to the world*, to see ourselves as an effect of "illusion of speculation" (Marx, 1988, p. 157) that is, the world of capitalist economy. Capital, product, labor – these are merely ideological constructs, a web which is thrown over everyday practice of life and deforms consciousness. We are, admittedly, victims of alienation, but given a different "representation" we will discern that we are also "the notorious crime of the whole of society" (Marx, 1982, p. 140). And as such, *we* also can change this situation.

Analogically, we could think about ideology in Wittgenstein's terms. One of the key and most intolerable features of ideology is that it always presents itself as *the only possible and inevitable* understanding of the reality. Wittgenstein's considerations on "aspects perception" enable us to present the concept of ideology in non-metaphysical terms. Wittgenstein reflects on "aspect change," "aspect dawning" and "aspect blindness" (Wittgenstein, 1986, pp. 193-201) within general question of relationship between seeing, thinking, and interpretation. Using schematic pictures like Jastrow's "duck-rabbit", Wittgenstein draws our attention to the situations when we are able to see one picture in many different ways/aspects, without any change within the picture itself. As a consequence we have to accept that our seeing is always "seeing as" and that our perception is always permeated with concepts. I suggest that Wittgenstein's analyses of aspect perception allow to defend ourselves against ideology, of which the most dangerous manifestation is aspect-blindness, and to release us from captivating us picture of ideology critique based on truth-reference. They help us "see pictures as pictures" (Norval, 2007, pp. 126-130) – that is, understand that what we perceive is never the real object or pure fact, but always *a picture*, and moreover that what we see as the picture depends on the way we arrange its elements. Furthermore, to experience the change of aspect is to be aware of the diversity of social and political reality, a diversity of understanding of our own situation. The experience of "aspect dawning" is irreversible; after such an experience, it is impossible to perceive the world as having only one aspect. We could refer to such experience as an emancipatory one: it helps us understand that the situation of domination we find ourselves in is not an ultimately fixed one, but rather, a confluence of historical and contingent processes whose constraints we experience (see Rasiński, 2018).

Filtered through the prism of Wittgenstein's critique of language, the Marxian idea of alienation and emancipation prompts us to conceive social criticism in non-foundationalist categories. Equally fruitful can be also a reverse move, that is, looking into Wittgenstein's categories from the perspective offered by the Marxian concept of emancipation.

Ferrucio Rossi-Landi, who was one of the first to notice affinities between Marx's and Wittgenstein's philosophical projects, aptly suggests that Wittgenstein's philosophy could be viewed as a therapy targeting specifically comprehended alienation which occurs at the level of language (Rossi-Landi, 1992, p. 100). Rupert Read addresses a similar phenomenon when he speaks of "parasitic language" (Read, 2002, p. 260) in Wittgenstein. We deal with it when an individual who uses language fails to achieve his/her goal. On such occasions, language becomes something alien to us and we cannot *express* what we wish by it, failing also, more importantly perhaps, to express *ourselves*. In *Investigations*, Wittgenstein portrays such an occurrence in following terms: "The confusions ... arise when language is like an engine idling, not when it is doing work" (Wittgenstein, 1986, § 132). Language is functional and it serves communication, information, description – "the engine" works then. Language fails to work when in its use its rules are violated, for example when we want to speak of something that cannot be an element of a language game or a form of life, that is, of something that cannot be "stirred" in practice. Theory (metaphysics) does not have a life of its own and, and as it is an illusion, it must rely on our everyday language to become real, much like a "capitalist" is parasitic upon a "worker" without being actually real. Wittgenstein calls it "a metaphysical language use" and clearly defines his philosophical task: "as bringing language back from its metaphysical to its everyday use". Bringing language "back" to itself could be understand as overcoming alienation, much as in Marx a return to oneself entails seeing through the apparent alienness of one's products.

In a way, Foucault's notion of genealogy brings together the Marxian idea of criticism and emancipation and the Wittgensteinian concept of "perspicuous representation".[11] As Owen suggests, in Foucault, thinking about power in categories of sovereignty exemplifies being held captive by a picture (*ibid.*, pp. 94-95). Aphoristic formulations about it feature abundantly in Foucault's interviews and lectures: "We need to cut off the King's head: in political theory that still needs to be done" (Foucault, 1980, p. 121), or "we have to abandon the model of Leviathan" (Foucault, 2003,

---

11   This analogy is noted, among others, by Owen (2007).

p. 34). The Leviathan symbolizes a model in which power is centrally invested in a state, law, government, and in which the most essential question is the legitimacy of power (see *ibid.*, p. 29). We have been locked up in such a framework of power practically since the Middle Ages, when juridical thought and royal power intertwined to mutually support and legitimize each other ever since. Foucault's prime goal is liberate us from this vision and, thereby, to foster our ability to govern ourselves. He pursues this goal by pitting a model of disciplinary power, or in broader terms biopower, against the model of sovereign power, which is supposed to help us shake off its "oppression". Revealing how, historically, the sovereignty-based model arose and developed helps us grasp how its picture has held us captive, affecting our thinking and constraining our capacity for self-government. Grasping our enslavement to the picture and the concomitant reduction of our freedom is, in turn, supposed to motivate us to engage in specific action to minimize the domination relationships that permeate "power games" in which we are entangled.

Foucault's idea of genealogy as "practical critique" (Foucault, 1984, p. 45) and the related concept of "technologies of the self" (see Foucault, 1988) could be approached in terms of both Marx's "emancipation" and Wittgenstein's "perspicuous representation". Foucault's genealogy relinquishes transcendentalism and universalism intrinsic to Kant's project, but at the same time it "opens up a space of freedom" (Foucault, 1998, p. 450) to us. Therefore it could be considered as a form of emancipatory practice and become an alternative to dominant model of critical theory based on rational agreement and argumentation. Foucault's practical critique is able to escape from something which can be described as "Habermas' blackmail":[12] Either we are accepting to some degree Kant's philosophical project, or we have to fall into irrationalism (Habermas, 2007, ch. IX, X.). On the one hand, it is able to avoid searching for foundations, which meets Wittgenstein's demand of philosophical therapy aimed at metaphysical use of language, and on the other hand it preserves in a way Marx's call for emancipation, evading however all the projects "that claim to be global or radical" (Foucault, 1984, p. 46).

Foucault describes his research as a "historical analysis of the limits that are imposed on us and an experiment with the possibility of going beyond them" (*ibid.*, p. 50). Clearly, there is no escaping historicity, and in this sense any criticism will be curbed and largely contingent – it will

---

12   I am referring here to Foucault's criticism of "blackmail of the Enlightenment" (see Foucault, 1984, pp. 42-45).

not be universal. That, nevertheless, helps us understand that neither are the constraints we experience: the conjuncture we find ourselves in is not an ultimately fixed one; rather, it is a confluence of contingent processes. It means that it is possible to think differently, that it is possible to "work" on oneself and thereby to make oneself "free" to a degree. In this sense, practical critique entails "an experimental attitude" that addresses one's own limitations because the very fact of capturing one's own conditioning opens opportunities for freedom, one which is palpable and involves "grasp[ing] the points where change is possible and desirable" (*ibid.*, p. 46). Practical critique is thus, first of all, work performed on oneself, a self-reflexive "technology of the self," or "an exercise of self upon self" [*exercise de soi sur soi*] (Foucault, 1987, p. 113), and presupposes possibilities of desubjugation [*désassujetissement*] (Foucault, 1997, p. 47).

Reading Marx through Wittgenstein reveals a *therapeutic* dimension of Marx's concepts which seeks to make us abandon the delusions of alienation, while in reading Wittgenstein through Marx, we come to see Wittgenstein's therapeutic investment in emancipatory categories. Both perspectives come together finally in Foucault's idea of genealogy, which, I believe, has both its emancipatory moment in critique that entails "not being governed quite so much" (*ibid.*, p. 45) and its therapeutic moment involved with Wittgenstein's "perspicuous representation." At the same time, I do not think that relinquishing the global perspective inherent in the Marxian vision abolishes the political dimension of Foucault's projects. Rather, I believe that his understanding of critique as *an emancipatory practice* ensues from a conviction that any global change is predicated upon earlier change in individual consciousness, a view that early Marx would readily have endorsed. In this sense, Foucault's project is not only deeply political, but also deeply democratic, because it does not reduce politics to a rational game of argumentation, but exposes the political in all identity formation processes in society.

References

Althusser L. (1994). Ideology and Ideological State Apparatuses. In S. Žižek (Ed.), *Mapping Ideology*. London, New York: Verso, pp. 100-140.
Apel K.O. (1980). *Towards a Transformation of Philosophy*. London, New York: Routledge.
Baker G. (2004). *Wittgenstein's Method: Neglected Aspects*, ed. by K. Morris. Oxford, Blackwell.

Benhabib S. (1984). The Marxian Method of Critique: Normative Presuppositions. *PRAXIS International* 3: 285, p. 284Ł-298.

Crary A. (2000). Wittgenstein's philosophy in relation to political thought. In A. Crary and R. Read (Eds.) *The New Wittgenstein*, pp. 118-146. London, New York: Routledge.

Dreyfus H., Rabinow P. (1983). *Michel Foucault: Beyond Structuralism and Hermeneutics*. University of Chicago Press.

Foucault M. (1980). Truth and Power. In M. Foucault, *Power/Knowledge: Selected Interviews and Other Writings 1972-1977*, ed. by Colin Gordon. New York: Pantheon Books, pp. 109-133.

Foucault M. (1984). What is Enlightenment? In P. Rabinow (Ed.), *The Foucault Reader*. New York: Pantheon Books, pp. 32-50.

Foucault M. (1987). The Ethic of Care for the Self as a Practice of Freedom (interview). In *Philosophy and Social Criticism*, vol. 12 , no 2-3, pp. 112-131.

Foucault M. (1988). Technologies of the Self. In Martin, L.H. et al (Eds.) *Technologies of the Self: A Seminar with Michel Foucault*. London: Tavistock, pp.16-49.

Foucault M. (1990). *The History of Sexuality*. Vol. 1, trans. Robert Hurley. New York: Vintage Books.

Foucault M. (1997). What is Critique? In S. Lotringer (Ed.), *The Politics of Truth. Michel Foucault.* trans. Lysa Hochroth, Catherine Porter Los Angeles: Semiotext(e), pp. 41-81.

Foucault M. (1998). Structuralism and Post-Structuralism. In J. Faubion (Ed.) trans. Robert Hurley et. al., *Aesthetics, method and epistemology. The Essential Works of Michel Foucault 1954-1984. Volume Two*. New York: The New Press, pp. 433-458.

Foucault M. (2003). *Society Must Be Defended: Lectures at College de France 1975-76*, ed. By M. Bertani and A. Fontana, trans. David Macey. New York: Picador.

Habermas J. (1974). Introduction: Some Difficulties in the Attempt to Link Theory and Praxis. In J. Habermas, *Theory and Practice.* trans. John Viertel. Boston: Beacon Press, pp. 1-40.

Habermas J. (1982). A Reply to my Critics. In J. B. Thompson, D. Held (Eds.), *Habermas: Critical Debates.* Cambridge: MIT Press, p. 219-283.

Habermas J. (1984). *Theory of Communicative Action. Volume I.* trans. Thomas McCarthy. Boston: Beacon Press.

Habermas J. (1990). Philosophy as Stand-In and Interpreter. In J. Habermas, *Moral Consciousness and Communicative Action*, trans. C. Lenhardt and S. Weber Nicholsen. Cambridge: MIT Press, pp. 1-20.

Habermas J. (1998*). Between facts and norms*, trans. W. Rehg. Cambridge: MIT Press.

Habermas J. (1999). Discourse Ethics. In J. Habermas, *Moral Consciousness and Communicative Action*, trans. C. Lenhardt and S. Weber Nicholsen. Cambridge: MIT Press, p. 43-115.

Habermas J. (2001). *On the Pragmatics of Social Interaction: Preliminary Studies in the Theory of Communicative Action*, trans. Barbara Fultner. Cambridge: MIT Press.

Habermas J. (2007). *The Philosophical Discourse of Modernity: Twelve Lectures*, trans. by Frederick Lawrence. Cambridge: Polity Press.

Hutchinson P., Read R. (2008). «Toward a Perspicuous Presentation of 'Perspicuous Presentation'», *Philosophical Investigations* 31, no. 2.

Hutto D. D. (2007). Getting Clear about Perspicuous Representations: Wittgenstein, Baker, and Fodor. In D. Moyal-Sharrock (Ed.), *Perspicuous Presentations: Essays on Wittgenstein's Philosophy of Psychology*. Basingstoke: Palgrave, pp. 299-322.

Kitching G., Pleasants N. (Eds.) (2002). *Marx and Wittgenstein. Knowledge, morality and politics*. London. New York: Routledge.

Marx K. (1982). *Critique of Hegel's Philosophy of Right*. Ed. and trans. Joseph O'Malley. Cambridge, Cambridge University Press.

Marx K. (1988). *Economic and Philosophic Manuscripts of 1844*. Trans. M. Milligan. New York, Prometheus Books.

Marx K. (1997). Exchange of Letters [letter to Ruge]. In K. Marx, *Writings of the young Marx on philosophy and society*. Ed. and trans. D. Easton and K.H. Guddat. Indianapolis: Hackett Publishing Company, Inc., pp. 203-215.

Mouffe C. (2000). *The Democratic Paradox*. London: Verso.

Mouffe C. (2013*). Agonistics: Thinking The World Politically*. London, New York: Verso.

Mouffe C. (2019). *For A Left Populism*. London, New York: Verso.

Norval A. (2007). *Aversive Democracy: Inheritance and Originality in the Democratic Tradition*. Cambridge: Cambridge University Press.

Owen D. (2007). Genealogy as Perspicuous Presentation. In J. H. Cressida (Ed.), *The Grammar of Politics: Wittgenstein and Political Philosophy*. Ithaca: Cornell University Press, pp. 82-96.

Rasiński L. (2018). 'A Picture Held Us Captive…' Marx, Wittgenstein and the 'Paradox of Ideology'. In L. Rasiński, D. Hill, K. Skordoulis (Eds.), *Marxism and Education. International Perspectives on Theory and Action*. London, New York: Routledge, pp. 133-143.

Read R. (2002). Marx and Wittgenstein on Vampires and Parasites: A Critique of Capital and Metaphysics. In G. Kitching, N. Pleasants (Eds.), *Marx and Wittgenstein. Knowledge, morality and politics*. London, New York: Routledge, p. 284-281.

Rosanvallon P. (2008). *Counter-Democracy: Politics in an Age of Distrust.* Cambridge University Press.

Rossi-Landi F. (1983). *Language as Work and Trade: A Semiotic Homology for Linguistics and Economy*, trans. by Martha Adams et al. South Hadley: Bergin & Garvey Publishers, Inc.

Rossi-Landi F. (1992). *Between Signs and Non-Signs*, ed. S. Petrilli. Amsterdam, Philadelphia: John Benjamins Publishing Company.

Rubinstein D. (1981). *Marx and Wittgenstein. Social Praxis and Social Explanation*. London: Routledge.

Sen A. (2003). Sraffa, Wittgenstein, and Gramsci. *Journal of Economic Literature* 41.

Tully J. (2008). *Public Philosophy in a New Key: Volume 1, Democracy and Civic Freedom*. Cambridge University Press.

Walzer M. (2006). *Politics and Passion. Toward a More Egalitarian Liberalism*. Yale University Press.

Weber M. (1978). *Economy and Society*. Ed. by G. Roth, K. Wittich. Berkeley, Los Angeles: University of California Press.

Wilson J., Swyngedouw E. (Eds.) (2014). *The Post-Political and Its Discontents. Spaces of Depoliticisation, Spectres of Radical Politics*. Edinburgh University Press.

Wittgenstein L. (1965). T*he Blue and Brown Books: Preliminary Studies for the 'Philosophical Investigations'*. New York: Harper and Row.

Wittgenstein L. (1975). *Zettel*, trans. G.E.M. Anscombe, ed. by G.E.M. Anscombe and G.H. von Wright. Berkeley, Los Angeles: University of California Press.

Wittgenstein L. (1986). *Philosophical Investigations*, trans. G.E.M. Anscombe. Oxford: Basil Blackwell.

Wittgenstein L. (1998). *Philosophical Remarks,* ed. by Rush Rhees, trans. by Raymond Hargreaves and Roger White. Oxford: Basil Blackwell.

Wittgenstein L. (2001). *Remarks on the foundations of mathematics*. Cambridge: MIT Press.

GAVIN KITCHING

SOCIAL SCIENCE AND THE 'AUGUSTINIAN PICTURE OF LANGUAGE'
A Fieldwork Experience and its Significance

1. *Introduction: Wittgenstein and Augustine*

(1)   When they (my elders) named some object, and accordingly moved toward something, I saw this and I grasped that the thing was called by the sound they uttered when they meant to point it out...Thus, as I heard words repeatedly used in their proper places in various sentences, I gradually learnt to understand what objects they signified; and after I had trained my mouth to form these signs, I used them to express my own desires.

(2)   If you describe the learning of language in this way you are, I believe, thinking of nouns like 'table', 'chair', 'bread' and of people's names and only secondarily of the names of certain actions and properties; and of the remaining kinds of word as something that will take care of itself. (Wittgenstein, 1972, p.2e)

You don't have to get beyond page 1 of Wittgenstein's *Investigations* to come across these words. Passage (1) is part of the quotation from Augustine's *Confessions* with which Wittgenstein begins his great book, and passage (2) is the beginning of his rejection of the "picture of the essence of human language" which he finds in the quotation.

And yet, while his placing of the Augustinian quotation, and his criticism of it, at the very beginning of the *Investigations* certainly seems to suggest its extreme importance to Wittgenstein, there has never been any agreement among commentators on *what* that importance is. For Wittgenstein surely cannot be saying (can he?) that speakers of a language (whether philosophers or others) are unaware that it is composed of words other than nouns. Or is he suggesting that native speakers treat *all* nouns as ontologically equivalent - think that words like 'energy', 'society', 'philosophy' or 'delusion' "name objects" of the same *kind* as those "named" by 'table', 'chair' or 'bread'? If so, this seems only slightly less insulting to their intelligence than their not knowing about pronouns, adverbs or adjectives. Certainly, I know of no native speaker of English or any other language who would deny a fundamental difference between abstract nouns and the names of common material objects and of people, even if they might struggle to describe that difference formally. And when it comes to philosophy, Wittgenstein surely *cannot* be suggesting that Plato or Aristotle (or Hegel or Kant or Descartes) thought all abstract nouns just functioned to name 'abstract objects', with the latter understood as simply 'insubstantial' versions of tables, chairs, pots, pans or Peters. If they did then their reputation, not just as philosophers but as intelligent men, would be entirely undeserved.

So if the 'Augustinian picture of language' is as profoundly misleading and as 'intelligence bewitching' as Wittgenstein appears to suggest it surely *cannot* be in any of these ways. Or can it?

2. *Wittgensteinian Philosophy and a Non-Philosopher*

There is a wealth of philosophical commentary on the above issue, (as on almost every other issue in the *Investigations*), and my aim here is not to add to that mass of words even if I thought there were anything new to say. My aim rather is to report the effect that a first reading of this remark (and the 28 or so which follow it) had on someone trained, *not* in Philosophy, but in Social Science, and in particular in Economics and Politics. Whatever they might have done to or for philosophers, for someone coming from a social science background, the first 29 or so remarks of the *PI* powerfully drew my attention to the central role that abstract nouns had played in my entire intellectual formation. For I had been taught Social Science almost entirely through the lens of such nouns. As a young economist I was taught that I was engaged in the scientific study of abstract 'things' such as Supply, Demand, Markets, Investment, Growth and Consumption etc. And as a would-be 'scientist' of Politics my goal was also to scientifically describe and explain yet more abstract objects, albeit different ones – Power, Authority, Sovereignty, Legitimacy, Democracy, Totalitarianism etc.

More importantly, the beginning of the *PI* drew my attention to the fact that the defining objects of social science disciplines were themselves abstract nouns. (Economics as the study of 'the Economy', Sociology as the study of 'Society' and Political Science as the study of 'Politics'.) And conceiving what, significantly, were called the 'objects of study' of social science in that way is simultaneously to conceive them from a certain perspective - the perspective of an outside observer. From the very beginning, my training in Economics and Political Science had always situated me intellectually and imaginatively *outside*, or *apart from*, 'the Economy' or 'Society'. And from that radically separated 'position' I had then to grasp such 'objects' both as abstract wholes *and* as wholes analysable into further abstract 'parts.'

Now to view any object from the outside is to view it from a distance, and the larger the object the greater the distance must be for it to appear *as* an 'object' at all. Thus, an intellectual perspective, just like a visual perspective, always simultaneously facilitates and impedes.   From Vermeer's landscape *View of Delft* we can learn a lot about the commercial and political life of the town, but almost nothing about the daily lives of its individual inhabitants. From his more typical 'interior' painting, *Young Woman Reading a Letter at an Open Window,* we can learn a lot about the latter, but only a little about the former.[1] Analogically, the higher the level of abstraction necessary to successfully grasp such 'objects' as 'total investment' or 'economic growth' or 'the total money supply' the less can be seen of the individual investment, savings and expenditure decisions which make up these magnitudes. And the high level of abstraction required to discuss the 'democratic legitimacy' of an entire 'political system' is one that entirely occludes individual political opinions or their formation.

It came as a revelation to me that in being linguistically socialised into two social science disciplines I had simultaneously been linguistically socialised into adopting an imagined perspective. But it came as even more of a revelation (and an enraging one) that I had been socialised in a way that had actively prevented me from understanding that. In essence, in presenting a particular perspective as the only 'scientific' or 'objective' perspective my social science education had completely hidden its own particularity. A rigidly *singular* conception of objectivity had rendered the perspectivity of social science invisible. I had been socialised into the belief that there is only *one* 'objectively correct' picture or representation of anything (a picture somehow determined by the object pictured), and that to question that was to question the hallowed concept of 'objectivity' itself.

Yet to understand an academic discipline perspectivally need not undermine belief in its objectivity. It simply points up that the social scientist, just like the visual artist, must *shift perspective* (must shift 'point

---

1   Or rather you can if you take the trouble to research the buildings in the landscape and the objects in the interior scene, as Timothy Brook does in his brilliant book (2008).

of view') depending on what it they *desire* to observe and analyse. To use another analogy, understanding the entire earth's ocean current system may require (among other things) the use of images from a satellite orbiting 100 miles above the planet. Understanding the current movements of the River Tiber may require (among other things) images taken from a satellite orbiting a lot closer to Earth and to Rome. Perspectively, there is always an 'objectively best' position from which to view anything. It is just that what is 'objectively best' cannot be specified separately from what one wishes to observe and understand – which means separately from one's purpose, or purposes, of study.

It would take me too far outside the concerns of this chapter to say, in detail, *how* I was taught a perspective non-perspectivally. But it should come as no surprise, conceptually speaking, that the prime means of doing it had been to focus my student attention entirely on what was *to be* observed, described and understood. (How does investment occur? How are supply and demand aligned and misaligned? How do democracies differ from totalitarian regimes? What are the major forms of political power?) and entirely away from the fact that 'I' (or some other subject – 'transcendental' or otherwise) was doing the observing, describing, explaining etc.

Even that rather understates or misstates the matter. For it was not so much that my attention was 'focused away' from any subjective dimension as that such a dimension was itself linguistically *abolished* or *annulled* by the use of passive forms of the verb[2]. In my social science education (and most especially in my economics education) abstract economic objects were always 'observed', 'explained', 'measured' and 'described' without anybody apparently *doing* the observing, explaining, measuring or describing. Hence it was entirely out of the question (out of the picture?) to ask who these observers or measurers were, 'where' they were, why they might be doing it, what they hoped to achieve by doing it, or whether indeed 'it' might be 'done' differently.

---

2   There is a further point about this and one that relates directly to my earlier discussion of the opening *PI* remark. When one speaks or writes entirely about a set of observations in complete occlusion of an actual or potential observer or observers, one tends, not merely to use passive forms of the verb a lot, one also tends to construct a prose which is heavy on nouns and adjectives but light on active forms of the verb and thus on adverbs and personal pronouns. I don't know whether Wittgenstein had something like this in mind in those first remarks about Augustine, but it is of interest nonetheless. 'Nouny' language does affect the pattern of use of "other kinds of words" in quite specific ways.

The above has been a non-philosopher's account of what he learnt philosophically about his own education and practice from Wittgenstein's remarks about the so-called 'Augustinian picture of language' - about the picture's temptations and traps, its epistemological emphases and occlusions. But it itself is only a 'general', 'broad' or 'abstract' philosophical account and one using an analogy – between intellectual perspectives and visual perspectives – which may also have hidden traps and complexities, may itself mislead as well as illuminate.

So I could at this point undertake yet more amateur philosophy and examine if, how and why the above analogy *might* mislead – how intellectual perspectives are like and unlike visual ones. But I am not going to do that now (although I shall come back to the issue) and for an impeccably pragmatic reason. For as a social scientist, the real importance for me of coming to conceive abstraction perspectivally, as a sort of 'point of view', was not philosophical – did not lie in its alleged philosophical advantages (coherence, subtlety, robustness to critique etc.) – but in its practical efficacy. In other words, my prime criterion for assessing the merits of a 'perspectival' approach to objectivity was pragmatic – whether it made me a better social science researcher.

My aim therefore in the next section of this chapter is to demonstrate, by reference to a piece of field research which I carried out in Russia in the late 1990s, how reconceiving my professional practice in this Wittgensteinian way *did* improve it. As we shall see, it did so in two ways. Firstly, it allowed me to recognise the *epistemological significance* of some empirical results of that research – results that I might otherwise have treated as 'unimportant' or 'marginal', or even have ignored entirely. Secondly, it helped me to recognise (as I probably would not have done without it) the crucial *epistemological weakness* in a crucial background literature debating whether rural Russian people 'were'/'are' peasants or not. Wittgenstein enabled to see that the substantive disagreements in this literature were less significant than the naively 'objectivist' assumptions, shared by *all* its contributors, about how that issue was to be determined.

But as we shall also see, these two Wittgenstein-derived improvements to my research practice were closely related. That is to say, my recognition of the limitations of a simply 'objectivist' approach to peasant identity, led me to see the significance of some field research results that I might otherwise have missed. But it was also my reflections on those results that provided the grounds or justifications for my critique of the 'Russian peasant' literature. And it is perhaps significant that I cannot now remember which of these insights came first – i.e. whether my reflections on 'naïve objectivism' of the Russian peasantry literature led me to 'see' some of our own field results differently, or whether, on the contrary, it was reflecting on the latter that led me to 'see' the 'Russian peasantry' debate differently. But perhaps posing the matter in this way is itself misleading. Perhaps neither of these insights came 'first'. Rather, my Wittgenstein-derived understanding of language *use*, sharpened my sensibilities to both these issues 'simultaneously'.

But in any case, all these matters should be clearer after the discussion of the Russian fieldwork experience and its philosophical implications which follows.

3. *'Peasants' in Russia*

Given the focus and likely audience of this book I will endeavour to keep the social science detail in what follows to a minimum. But a certain amount of it and of contextual scene setting is necessary for comprehension of the subsequent philosophical discussion, so I ask for readers' indulgence.

In the northern hemisphere summers of 1996 and 1997, I was engaged, along with some colleagues from the University of Moscow, on a field investigation of the progress (or lack thereof) of the 'decollectivisation' of Russian agriculture. This was the attempt, following the collapse of the USSR, to decrease the amount of the country's agricultural production coming from 'state' and 'collective' farms and to increase that coming from newly-established private farms. This Soros-Foundation-funded project was carried out in four regions of European Russia (Vologda, Vladimir, Tver and Orel). It involved the administering of standardised questionnaires to state and collective farm chairmen and administrators, to ordinary farm workers or labourers, and to some of the newly independent private farmers. It also involved conducting more detailed semi-structured interviews with smaller sub-samples of all these groups, interviews which covered a broader range of social and political questions than the rather narrowly economistic survey questionnaires.

On completion, a lengthy 'team' report of our findings was sent to Soros, but I also used some of those findings in three articles I wrote for the *Journal of Peasant Studies* and the *Journal of Agrarian Change* (Cfr. Kitching, 1998a, pp.1-30; 1998b, pp.43-81; and 2001, pp.57-80). As part of my broader reading for these I came across a Soviet-era debate about whether, despite collectivisation, the population of rural Russia could still be regarded as peasants. This debate arose from the fact that, throughout the Soviet period, the mass of state and collective farm workers continued to depend for their subsistence on food grown on the small 'private plots' made available to them by the collectives. This subsistence consisted not just of food grown on the plot and directly consumed, but also of small amounts of money obtained from selling surpluses of 'private plot' crops and animal products (eggs, meat, milk) on local markets. This debate interested me because, for reasons which do not need to be discussed here, our research had revealed that in the immediate post-Soviet period most people in rural Russia had become even *more* dependent on their private plots for their survival. Moreover, the Russian urban population had become even more reliant on buying private-plot-produced food than it had been under Communism. In short, a kind of 're-peasantisation' of Russian agriculture and food supply seemed to be occurring, in both rural and urban areas, in the immediate aftermath of the collapse of the USSR.

The contributors to the debate about the Russian peasantry divided into two broad groups, those taking a broadly Marxian approach, and those using an understanding of 'Peasant Economy' deriving from the work of the great Russian agronomist A.V. Chayanov.[3] Some of those disposed to the Chayanovian view also combined it with an interest in the broader cultural characteristics of peasants – their forms of family and kinship organisation, religious or magical beliefs, 'localist' and anti-urban values, etc.

So, for example, Ian Hill, in a well-known contribution dating from the mid-1970s, characterised a peasantry as "an ideal type of social formation" distinguished by four features:

(1) a *"traditional culture"* involving a tight knit "moral community" of "the village", and a predominantly oral culture combining traditional "folk" elements such as spiritual and magical beliefs, with some externally-introduced elements of an urban "high' culture, such as basic literacy and numeracy.

(2) A *"family-based agricultural subsistence economy"* using an "economic logic" somewhat at odds with market logic. [The Chayanovian conception of the peasantry]

---

3   A.V.Chayanov (1966). Despite his socialist convictions Chayanov died in a labour camp because, at the height of the Stalinist collectivisation and 'anti-kulak' campaigns of the 1930s, he committed the sin of suggesting that peasants were not capitalists or even proto-capitalists but operated according to a distinctively peasant economic logic. In particular, unlike capitalist farmers, they had a culturally fixed standard of living, so they actually worked and produced *less* when prices of their products rose and they could obtain that standard with less 'drudgery'. This was the so-called 'backward-sloping supply curve' of peasant labour.

(3) A *social structure* in which economic production is deeply interred in *"family and kin relations"* and in which those relations deeply "mediate" the peasant's relations with the wider world and especially with the state.

(4) *A lack of ramified political organisation beyond the family and village.* This stems from features (2) and (3) and makes peasant mass mobilisation difficult unless it is led and organised by non-peasant urban groups (Hill, 1975, pp. 109-27).[4]

As against this kind of Chayanovian/Weberian approach, focused predominantly on what peasants ideal typically "are" or what a peasantry ideal typically "is", the Marxian contributors to this debate tended to focus not on Russian peasants *per se,* but on the relationship of peasant production to industrial and 'market-mediated' forms of production and consumption. As I said in one of the articles:

> ...Marxist theorists have predominantly approached the peasant and the peasantry in a structural way, which makes what the peasant is *not,* more important than what she or he is...the most important thing about peasants...is that they are not, in the sense intended by Marx, 'workers.' That is, peasants do not subsist by selling their 'free' labour power to a capitalist class, but rather by using means of production in land...to produce and reproduce their own labour power. This...means that peasants are often of restricted utility to a capitalist class as consumers as well as producers...whereas workers are entirely dependent on their wages...for their subsistence and are therefore...constrained to consume the products of capital as well as...to produce them, peasants tend not to work much for capitalists nor to consume much of what they produce... they tend therefore to be a 'brake' on the rapid spread and development of the capitalist mode of industrial production. (Kitching, 1998b, p.49)

For reasons which may now be evident, scholars taking this Marxist approach tended to conclude that, despite their possession of private plots and dependence on such plots for part of their subsistence, the people of rural Russia were *not* peasants at all. Because in the Soviet and post-Soviet periods, most of their labour time was expended on state or collective farms and they were also significant consumers of the products of Soviet industry. And in the post-Soviet period they had become consumers of foreign manufactures as well. In Marxian jargon, Russian rural people had been "substantively subsumed" to non-peasant forms of production and thus were no longer peasants. The view of the Chayanovians and of 'synthetic'

---

4   This summary is of pp.110-11 of his article.

theorists like Hill however, was that *sovkhoz* and *kolkhoz* workers[5] were still essentially peasants because of their continued dependence on small-scale subsistence and commercial production, and because of their other 'peasant-like' social and cultural characteristics.[6]

However, despite this theoretical division and the opposed conclusions to which it led, I was more impressed by what all the participants in the debate about the Russian peasantry had in common than by what divided them. Because the unstated assumption of *all* of them was that whether rural Russian people "were" or "were not" peasants was something to be entirely determined by them – the Chayanovians, or the Marxists, or the 'synthetic culturalist' theorists like Hill. And it was to be determined *entirely* by whether rural Russian people met, or did not meet, certain 'objective' criteria of 'peasantness' – the theoretical disagreement being only over what those criteria were and/or over how different criteria were to be weighted.

Although it is very difficult to be sure of these things retrospectively, I think I probably could have made this critique of the 'Russian peasantry' literature – as based in an unreconstructed and naïve 'objectivism' - (to use David Rubinstein's term (1981, especially chapter 2, pp.27-61)) whether or not I had read any Wittgenstein. What I could *not* have done without the *PI* however, was to see the epistemological significance of some very different uses of the Russian terms for 'peasant' and 'peasants '(*krest'ian* and *krest'iani*) appearing in my field diaries and in the transcriptions of our semi-structured interviews. These uses were found not only in the statements of rural Russian people, but also in the conversations occurring *among* the researchers themselves, (conversations which I had noted in my field diaries).

Since it is impossible to discuss the philosophical (or political) implications of those uses without first presenting them to readers, there follows a lengthy verbatim extract from the *Journal of Peasant Studies* article in which I excerpted some of those interviews and conversations. The passage also includes some of my initial reflections on those excerpts.

1. *Interviewer* (to a collective farm chairman) 'How would you describe your social origins?'

---

5   '*Sovkhoz'* is the Russian term for a state farm, '*kolkhoz'* the term for a collective farm. There were, and are, differences between the two but they are not relevant to the discussion here.

6   Actually, Hill reached somewhat uncertain or ambiguous conclusions about this. See Kitching 1998b, pp.46-7 for broader comments.

Farm Chairman 'Oh local and peasant. Like a lot of other leaders around here.'

2. *Irena K.* (A Russian colleague to me, contemptuously, after the completion of an interview with an elderly ex-collective farm chairman). 'That last guy was a typical kolkhoznik. He has a typical kolkhoznik mentality, not like that old lady – Christina – whom we interviewed last week. Remember her?'

G.K. 'Yes, but what do you mean – "a typical kolkhoznik"? And what did you mean when you said that Christina had "a typical peasant mentality". What does that mean?'

Irena K. 'It means that he simply cannot conceive life in the countryside without kolkhozes and sovkhozes, and in fact he is afraid of what it would mean. But Christina enjoys her independence, likes looking after her animals, and feels confident she could manage whether the kolkhoz was there or not.'

3. *(A farm chairman, Orel region)* 'The peasants will always survive. I know them, I was born among them. As long as you have a bit of land and a few animals you can always survive, whatever happens to the economy. But without the help they get from the kolkhozes and sovkhozes they'd find it a lot tougher and they know that.'[7]

4. *(A farm accountant, also Orel region)* 'People are a lot more civilised in the countryside these days. They take a lot of things for granted – cars, transport, education, housing. They're not like the old peasants. They're not used to really tough times.'

In these quotations we find the word 'peasant' and its derivatives being *used* to:

(a) make a claim for local identification and social belonging (quotation 1). The claim needs to be made just because the person making it occupies a superior ('non-peasant') role in the local social structure but is claiming that this does not prevent him understanding and identifying with those 'below' him in this structure.

(b) stress a certain social distance, whilst still claiming local knowledge and familiarity (quotation 3). The comment at (a) above also applies here, but in a slightly different way.

---

7   Throughout the Soviet period, and even more in the early 'post-Soviet' years, many state and collective farms supported private plot production by allowing their workers to use state-owned equipment and transport to produce and market private plot output. That is what the Orel farm chairman is referring to here. This 'symbiosis' between the state and collective farms and private plot production had, and has, many other economic and social implications which cannot be explored here. For a discussion see Kitching (1998b, pp.52-67).

(c) designate a difference in attitude and behaviour found among rural Russian people and express an urban intellectual's approval of one pattern and disdain for the other (quotation 2)

(d) describe a degree of social and cultural change (even 'progress'?) while expressing worry about the psychological concomitants of that change – the loss of a certain toughness – which might be costly in the difficult future facing rural Russian people in the post-Soviet period. Here explicitly, and implicitly in quotation 2 as well, the peasant people of old Russia are seen as having been much less 'civilised', but just for that reason better able to cope when times get tough and a lot of the gains of civilisation are taken away or eroded. (*Ibid.,* pp.47-8)

What struck me most forcibly in reflecting on these exchanges was that all these uses of the terms 'peasant' and 'peasants' were essentially *expressive* rather than descriptive. That is, they either expressed the desire of some non-peasant people for a relationship with peasants (a desire sometimes based on having a peasant family background, or at least some 'insider' knowledge of peasants, sometimes on a frank 'outsider' admiration for the virtues or supposed virtues of 'real' peasants) or they expressed worries or concerns about the future of Russian rural people in the post-Soviet period.

More than that however, in our interviews with *kolkhoz* and *sovkhoz* workers (with the 'peasants' themselves) they *also* used the terms *krest'ian* and *krest'iani* of themselves in ways expressive as well as descriptive. In their case however they were mainly expressing their deep *resentment* at being peasants at all. They readily asserted that they *were* peasants, and 'proud' to be so, but said that their state or collective farm wages were so low that they were left with no choice but to engage in 'part-time peasanting' to supplement both their diets and their meagre cash incomes. And they left us in no doubt who they blamed for this, the Communist state in general and its local institutions and functionaries in particular (the *kolkhozes* and *sovkhozes* chairmen and other administrators – the 'non-peasant' outsiders in the Russian countryside.) As I observed, the *kolkhoz* and *sovkhoz* workers whom we interviewed proudly self-identified as peasants as way of expressing "a bitterly subordinated anti-state localism", as a way of making a kind of ideological and moral virtue out of a state-imposed necessity (*ibid.,* p.51).

But whether the terms '*krest'ian*' and '*krest'iani*' were being used to express the feelings of 'outsiders' about Russian rural people, or by those people themselves to express their resentment at an imposed fate, what struck me on reflection was that they were not *simply* being used as the theorists used them - to describe a set of economic or social *characteristics* (small-scale subsistence farming, use of family labour, 'backward-sloping supply curves' of labour, possession of a 'folk' culture, centrality of kinship relations, 'traditional' or magical 'belief structures' etc.) And this led me to some further philosophical reflections to which I now turn.

4. *Philosophy Post-Fieldwork*

The first point to make is that none of these experiences led me to conclude that 'objectivist' conceptions of the peasantry were 'wrong' while a Wittgenstein-derived 'expressive' conception was 'right'. Rather this Russian fieldwork only reinforced my conviction, expressed in the first part of this chapter, that any philosophically defensible concept of objectivity must be *purpose-dependent,* that the 'objectively best' conception of anything is dependent on one's purposes in conceiving and/or observing. That I had found expressive uses of the terms *krest'ian'* and *'krest'iani'* apparently unknown in, or just ignored by, the objectivist peasant literature did not mean that literature was totally worthless. For there were, and are, perfectly acceptable purposes for which a 'Chayanovian' or a Marxist or a 'synthetic-culturalist' conception of the peasantry might be the 'objectively best' conception to adopt.

But, and to return to an issue I previously raised only to side-step, those same expressive uses of peasant terminology did show me something philosophically new. They showed me that the analogising of different views of 'Society' to different visual perspectives *does* have limitations, that there *are* ways in which it itself is misleading or occluding. For whereas Vermeer could really stand at a spatial distance from Delft to view it as an object in a landscape, and satellites can really orbit 100 miles above the earth to provide images of ocean currents, the social scientist can only imaginatively 'stand outside' 'Society' to view it as an object. In reality every social scientist is always *in* a particular society and, over most of her/his actual life, is thinking, speaking and writing not as an 'observer' of some gargantuan abstract object 'out there' but as a *participant in* small-scale and immediate social relations.

Thus the expressive uses of the words 'peasant' and 'peasants' which we heard *and ourselves engaged in* in the Russian countryside are importantly misconceived if thought of as embodying some radically different perspective on the peasantry to that used by the objectivist theorists. Because actually the *sovkhoz* and *kolkhoz* workers we interviewed often expressed their resentment at being part-time peasants *at the same time and in the same sentences* in which they described 'objectively' what such peasanting involved – the enormously long hours of labour entailed in being a *kolkhoz* worker *and* a peasant; the hard work involved in tending their private plot crops and animals; the particularly onerous demands placed on women 'worker-peasants' because, as well as doing collective *and* private plot agricultural work they also had the bulk of domestic labour to perform; etc.[8] In other words, the part-time peasants of rural Russia often described themselves as peasants in ways which the objectivist theorists would instantly have recognised and approved *at the same time as – and indeed as an important means of –* expressing their deep resentment of their situation. Within the Russian countryside, description and expression were not two radically different 'perspectives', to be analogised to two different artistic 'views' or 'points of view'. On the contrary, expression was often occurring through description and as part of description.

But this is just what Wittgenstein saw in the *PI*, and just what all objectivist social science theories and theorists fail to grasp – that in the lives of people *in* society there are no 'purely descriptive' or 'purely explanatory' uses of language. And that is not because people do not describe things or explain things, but because they are nearly always (always?) doing other things *while* they are describing and/or explaining. This also means that there is an important philosophical difficulty with another distinction beloved of objectivist theorists – between describing or explaining something 'objectively' on the one hand and evaluating it 'subjectively' on the other. The difficulty simply is that *in* society (as against some imaginative position 'outside' it) describing is often (also) evaluating, explaining is often (also) evaluating, and that is shown not only in what people say but in the tone of voice in which they say it and in the facial expressions that accompany what they say.

I do not know whether Wittgenstein intended us to grasp all this from those famous opening remarks on the Augustinian picture. But I do know that conceiving language as simply, or even primarily, a set of 'labels' which one sticks on the world, is a conception which can only even seem plausible from a 'point of view' which is as deeply alienated as it is imaginary. And there was a time when some Marxists also knew this, when what they would have called the 'dialectic' between observer and observed and between observation of the world and action in it was

---

8   For more details, and some excerpts from our interviews with rural Russian people concerning their experience of 'part-time peasanting' (*ibid.,* pp.59-60).

central to their whole world view[9]. But sadly, over my life at least, far too much self-described 'Marxist' theorising has become just another form of objectivism, obsessed with trying, in a kind of purposeless vacuum, to prove the superiority of Marxist descriptions and explanations of the world over various 'bourgeois' alternatives.[10]

There was a time when I too was prey to such conceptions, and I was rescued from them only by a - largely accidental and fortuitous – exposure to the later Wittgenstein[11]. But 'structuralist', 'realist' or 'positivistic' accounts of Marx and Marxism ('scientistic' accounts as I would now call them) are not the only routes into objectivist alienation, and an exposure to Wittgenstein is not the only way to escape that alienation. But it is perhaps the most intellectually brilliant, elegantly expressed and (above all) deeply human escape route offered in modern philosophy[12]. For as the young Marx taught, at bottom alienation is alienation from one's own humanity, and to read the later Wittgenstein is to be *made* to recognise his humanity, and one's own through his. And one does that, (just as in the case of listening to those 'expressively describing' Russian rural people), by responding both to what he says *and* how he says it.

References

Brook T. (2008) *Vermeer's Hat: The Seventeenth Century and the Dawn of the Global World*. London: Profile.

Chayanov A. V. (1966). *The Theory of Peasant Economy*, ed. by D. Thorner, B. Kerblay and R.E.F.Smith. Homewood, Illinois: American Economic Association.

Kitching G. (1998a). The Development of Agrarian Capitalism in Russia 1991-97: Some Observations from Fieldwork, *Journal of Peasant Studies*, Vol 25, No 3, April 1998, pp.1-30,

---

9   I am thinking here of the Lukács of *History and Class Consciousness,* of the Korsch of *Marxism and Philosophy*, and of Horkheimer, Adorno and the early Frankfurt School, as well as of the early Marx.

10   For a more detailed discussion, see Kitching (2002, pp.232-53).

11   See Kitching (2003, pp.1-24), for a detailed account of my largely serendipitous encounter with Wittgenstein and its background.

12   An observation first brilliantly made in 1966 by Ferrucio Rossi-Landi in his "Toward a Marxian Use of Wittgenstein", a shortened version of which is in (Kitching and Pleasants, 2002, pp.185-212). Unfortunately, Rossi-Landi's subsequent development of a kind of 'linguistic' Marxism tended to revert to a rather undialectical objectivism. For a discussion see Israel (2002, pp.213-27).

Kitching G. (1998b). The Revenge of the Peasant? The Collapse of Large-Scale Russian Agriculture and the Role of the Peasant 'Private Plot' in that Collapse 1991-97, *Journal of Peasant Studies,* Vol 26, No 1, October 1998, pp.43-81

Kitching G. (2001). The Concept of *Sebestoimost'* in Russian Farm Accounting: A Very Unmagical Mystery Tour, *Journal of Agrarian Change,* Vol 1, No.1, January 2001, pp.57-80

Kitching G. (2002). Marxism and Reflexivity. In G. Kitching and N. Pleasants (Eds.) *Marx and Wittgenstein; Knowledge, Morality and Politics.* London: Routledge, 2002, pp.232-53.

Kitching, G. (2003). A Structuralist Marxist Meets the Later Wittgenstein. In *Wittgenstein and Society: Essays in Conceptual Puzzlement.* Aldershot: Ashgate, pp.1-24,

Kitching G. and Pleasants N. (Eds). (2002). *Marx and Wittgenstein; Knowledge, Morality and Politics.* London: Routledge.

Hill I. (1975). The End of the Russian Peasantry: The Social Structure and Culture of the Contemporary Soviet Agricultural Population, *Soviet Studies*, Vol 27, No 1, January 1975, pp. 109-27.

Israel J. (2002). Remarks on Marxism and the Philosophy of Language. In G. Kitching and N. Pleasants (Eds), *Marx and Wittgenstein; Knowledge, Morality and Politics.* London: Routledge, pp.213-27.

Rossi-Landi F. (1966). Toward a Marxian Use of Wittgenstein. In G. Kitching and N. Pleasants (Eds), *Marx and Wittgenstein; Knowledge, Morality and Politics.* London: Routledge, 2002, pp.185-212.

Rubinstein D. (1981). *Marx and Wittgenstein: Social Praxis and Social Explanation.* London: Routledge & Kegan Paul.

Wittgenstein L. (1972). *Philosophical Investigations.* Oxford: Basil Blackwell.

CONTRIBUTORS

FELICE CIMATTI is full professor of Philosophy of Language at the University of Calabria. His latest books are: A Biosemiotic Ontology: The Philosophy of Giorgio Prodi (2018) and Unbecoming Human: Philosophy of Animality After Deleuze (2020).

MOIRA DE IACO is Ajdunct Professor of Language Education at the University of Bari "Aldo Moro". She is author of several articles and monographies on Wittgenstein's philosophy of language. She investigated Sraffa's influence on Wittgenstein. Among her last scientific works there are the book *Wittgenstein e Sraffa* (Aracne, 2020) and the contributions "Wittgenstein to Sraffa: Two newly-discovered letters from February and March 1934" (NWR, 2019), "A List of Meetings between Wittgenstein and Sraffa" (NWR, 2018), "Sraffa and Wittgenstein. Steinvorth's testimony, letters and documents" (Paradigmi, 2018).

CHRISTOPH DEMMERLING is Professor of Philosophy at the Friedrich Schiller University Jena. The philosophy of emotions, philosophy of language, and the history of philosophy in the 20th century are his main research interests. He has published essays on critical theory, phenomenology, hermeneutics and analytical philosophy. He is author of *Sprache und Verdinglichung. Wittgenstein, Adorno und das Projekt einer kritischen Theorie* (1994), co-author of *Grundprobleme der analytischen Sprachphilosophie. Von Frege zu Dummett* (1998), author of *Sinn, Bedeutung, Verstehen. Untersuchungen zu Sprachphilosophie und Hermeneutik* (2002), co-author of *Philosophie der Gefühle. Von Achtung bis Zorn* (2007), and co-editor of *Deutsche Zeitschrift für Philosophie*.

DIMITRIS GAKIS is a research fellow at the Institute of Philosophy, KU Leuven, Belgium. He received his PhD degree from the Faculty of Humanities, University of Amsterdam, The Netherlands in 2012. From 2016 until 2018 he was a Marie Skłodowska Curie postdoctoral fellow at the Institute of Philosophy, KU Leuven, Belgium. His research interests include Wittgenstein, (post-)Marx(ism) and radical political theory, metaphilosophy, and biopolitics. He has published, among others, on the political aspects of Wittgenstein's philosophy and the connections between Wittgenstein and Marx(ism) in journals such as *Philosophy & Social Criticism* and *Constellations*. He currently works on the intersection of Wittgenstein's philosophy and radical political theory aiming to develop a Wittgensteinian biopolitical analysis and critique of late capitalism.

PIETRO GAROFALO studied Philosophy at the Università della Calabria and obtained his PhD from the Philosophy Department of the Università degli Studi di Palermo in 2014. He has been Visiting PhD at the Westfälische Wilhelms Universität Münster (2012) and at the Goethe-Universität Frankfurt (2013). He is a member of the editorial boar of Rivista italiana di filosofia del linguaggio (RIFL) and has edited *Frammenti di realtà sociale* (2015), co-edited (with M. Quante) *Lo spettro è tornato. Attualità della filosofia di Marx* (2017). His research interests include philosophy of language, social philosophy and social ontology.

GAVIN KITCHING was born in 1947, grew up in the English coal mining village of Fencehouses, County Durham and attended Washington Grammar School. He was awarded a Bsc (Econ) in Economics and Politics at Sheffield University in 1968 and an Oxford D.Phil in African Studies in 1972. He was a Fulbright Fellow at the State University of New York in the 1980s, has held held university posts in England, Wales, the USA, Canada and Kenya, and has conducted agrarian fieldwork research in Tanzania, Kenya, Brazil and Russia. He has been a Professor of Politics at the University of New South Wales, Sydney, Australia since 2004. He is now an Emeritus Professor there, and a Fellow of the Australian Academy of Social Sciences. His highly regarded corpus of work spans the disciplines of economics, politics, history and the later philosophy of Ludwig Wittgenstein.

LOTAR RASIŃSKI is the Associate Professor of Philosophy at the University of Lower Silesia in Wroclaw, Poland, and at Palacky University, Olomouc, Czech Republic. He held post-doctoral fellowships at New School for Social Research in New York and the University of California at Berkeley. For his latest book, *In the Footsteps of Marx and Wittgenstein. Social Criticism without Critical Theory* (in Polish; 2012) he received the prestigious Award of the Prime Minister of Poland (2014). In his research and publications he focuses on political philosophy, theory of discourse, critical theory, philosophy of social science and philosophy of education. His books include, *Discourse and Power. Exploring Political Agonism*, (in Polish; 2010), *Language, Discourse, Society. Linguistic Turn in Social Philosophy* (ed., in Polish; 2009) and *Marxism and Education. International Perspectives on Theory and Action* (with D. Hill, K. Skordoulis, eds.; 2018).

GUIDO SEDDONE is associate professor of Theoretical Philosophy at the University of Sassari and Marie-Curie Fellow. His main interests lie in social philosophy, self-consciousness, practical philosophy, American pragmatism, Hegel and Wittgenstein. He is author of *Stufen des Wir* (2011), *Collective Intentionality, Norms and Institutions* (2014), *Condivisione ed Impegno* (2015). He is also the editor of *Mind, Collective Agency, Norms* (2017) and of *Naturalism and Normativity in Hegel's Philosophy* (2019).

MIMESIS GROUP
www.mimesis-group.com

MIMESIS INTERNATIONAL
www.mimesisinternational.com
info@mimesisinternational.com

MIMESIS EDIZIONI
www.mimesisedizioni.it
mimesis@mimesisedizioni.it

ÉDITIONS MIMÉSIS
www.editionsmimesis.fr
info@editionsmimesis.fr

MIMESIS COMMUNICATION
www.mim-c.net

MIMESIS EU
www.mim-eu.com

Printed by
Digital Team – Fano (PU)
January 2022